More Praise
The Pou

"Manny Goldman has done a great job of gathering some of the greatest minds in Personal Growth to support you on your journey. His work represents the next generation of thought leaders in our field. This book is fun, simple and easy to read. Put this book at your beside. Enjoy it first thing in the morning and as the last thing you read at night."
~ Scott Martineau, CEO, ConsciousOne.com and
#1 Best Selling Author, *The Power of YOU!*

"*The Power of Personal Growth* is the seed that will impact billions of people. By reading this book and passing it on, you will impact your life, the life of your loved ones and the global community. Personal Growth is transforming the world one person at a time. "
~ Roger Hamilton, Chairman, XL Results Foundation

"This book will become your companion on the path to Personal Growth. It's packed with uplifting stories that will encourage you to tap your inner renegade, stretch your definition of success, and keep you going on the tough days."
~ Christine Comaford-Lynch, Author of the NY Times Best-seller *Rules for Renegades* and the CEO of Mighty Ventures

"Are you struggling in life? Then get this book, *The Power of Personal Growth*. It brilliantly shows you the key insights and wisdom for living. All you need to do is apply will power to the formula and your life will never be the same!"
~ Ken D. Foster, Author, *Ask and You Will Succeed* and
CEO, Shared Vision Network

"*The Power of Personal Growth* should be a required textbook for every child in school. Personal Growth, as explained in this book, is the heart and soul of achievement, success and happiness in life. I became a millionaire at the age of 29 because I was exposed to these exact concepts and strategies in my early adult life. For anyone looking for a strategy that is guaranteed to accelerate your level of success, The Power of Personal Growth is a must read."
~ Matt Morris, Author and Founder, SuccessUniversity.com

Manny Goldman has connected the power of Personal Growth with loving and caring for yourself and your family. The wisdom and insights shared in this book will enrich you and your loved ones for years to come.
~ Loren Slocum, Author of *The Greatest Love*
and *Getting Your Groove Back*

Present for:

From:

Date:

Special Message:

THE POWER OF PERSONAL GROWTH

Key Insights and Wisdom for Living

MANNY GOLDMAN

www.PersonalGrowth.com

Published by Personal Growth Press, Inc.
406 Broadway Suite 150A
Santa Monica, CA 90401

The Power of Personal Growth
by Manny Goldman

Copyright © 2008 Personal Growth Press, inc.

All Rights Reserved.

Cover and text design: Susie Ward, The Admin Source, Inc.

First printing January, 2008
ISBN 978-0-9802101-0-1

Additional copies of this book may be purchased at a discount for educational, business, or sales promotional use by contacting the publisher at 406 Broadway Suite 150A, Santa Monica, CA 90401.

visit www.PersonalGrowth.com

This book is dedicated to my loving wife, Vania, our families, friends and everyone who supported me throughout my life.

Acknowledgments

There are so many amazing people in my life who have played a part in the creation of this book. So much time, energy, and effort goes into a project of this nature. It could have never happened without the help of so many people.

First and foremost, this book would not have been possible without guidance and inspiration from my Higher Power. Some may call it God, the Divine, Spirit, or the Universe. To me, they are all one and the same. I truly believe and know that this book was a gift. I am extremely grateful to be the receiver.

My parents, Allan and Doris Goldman, have played an integral part in who I am and where I'm going. Throughout the years, they have made sacrifices to provide me with the best life they could. I am forever grateful for their never-ending support, encouragement and extreme generosity.

I am blessed with and thank my beautiful and amazing wife, Vania Goldman. Having her in my life makes me the luckiest person in the world. Vania loved me before my Personal Growth journey—and that wasn't an easy thing to do. Her continuing support, love, and belief in who I am and what I am doing are critical to my success.

I am also extremely grateful to my brother, Mark, and his girlfriend, Deanna; my sister, Vicki, and her life partner, Erica; my nieces, Alexa and Lilian; my grandmothers and all three grandfathers who are no longer with us; my aunts, uncles, and cousins; my in-laws, Manuel and Fatima Delgado, sister-in-law Cecilia Delgado, god-daughter Isabella and the rest of Vania's amazing family. I also want to thank my friends who have touched my heart throughout my life. They all bring me much joy and fuel my passion to live my dreams.

Without the following group of people and companies, I would not have been able to conceive this project. I would like to thank my teachers: Anthony Robbins, T. Harv Eker, Landmark Education, Robert Kiyosaki, Chris Howard, Clinton Swaine, Steven S. Sadleir, James Ray, David Deida, Jack Canfield, Les Brown, Mark Victor Hansen, Brian Tracy, Alex Mandossian, Jay Abraham, Joel and Heidi Roberts, Blair Singer, Keith Cunningham, Jim Rohn, Sarano Kelley, Pat Finn, Dr. Lin Morel, Bill Bartmann, Lynn Rose, Joseph Faust, David Wolmack, Nada Adams, Denis Waitley, Napoleon Hill, Dr. Colbey Forman, Kim Castle, and many others. As you can tell, I am an avid student of Personal Growth.

There is one person directly involved that stands out in the crowd—Jennifer S. Wilkov. Without her guidance, contacts, support, and efforts, *The Power of Personal Growth* would never have materialized. Jennifer is a dear friend and the book consultant for the project. Thank you so very much, Jennifer, for who you are, what you stand for, and what you do in this world.

Other very significant people directly and indirectly involved in the project whom I want to thank are: David Sendroff, Korby Waters, Angela Hartman, Ed Ernsting, Susie Ward, Gregg Corella, Spike Humer, Bret Dabe, Ira Goldman, Henrietta Cohen, Charles Debenedittis, Jr., Rod Nunez, Pat Finn, Kathryn Arnold, Keith Johnson, Mike Heu, Paul Hoffman, Payson Cooper, Eric Lamb, Peter McGreevy, Becky Dielman, Erik S., Mikae Pilaprat, Otto Ruebsamen, Joseph Varghese, Daniel Topkis, Brenda Zimbardi, Richard Duszczak, Stephanie and Greg Mulac and Mark Katz.

I want to personally thank those extraordinary people who purchased the book before it was formally released. Without them, this book may have not been possible. These people believe in me and my mission. For that, I am forever grateful.

Special thanks go out to the amazing people, who were interviewed for *The Power of Personal Growth*. If you go to pages

97 through 99, I have listed each of them. These people have a unique place in my heart and I am extremely grateful to have connected with them.

And finally, my deepest appreciation is to you, dear reader: I honor and respect you for your courage to pursue Personal Growth in your life, and for making the decision to join us in creating a compelling future for your life, your loved ones and the world.

I'm looking forward to spending time with all of you in the near future as we continue to raise the global awareness of the power of Personal Growth for billions of people.

In this picture taken
October 2nd, 2004 I was...
- *245lbs*
- *Clinically depressed*
- *$100,000 in debt*
- *Lost with what to do
  with my life*

In this picture taken
September 4th, 2005 I was...
- *190lbs*
- *Extremely happy
  about my life*
- *Financially stable*
- *Clear about my
  purpose in life*

These pictures are only 11 months apart

In this book, I share my story of how Personal Growth transformed my life and the key insights and wisdom that made all the difference for me.

Contents

Introduction

You are about to embark on an exploration into *The Power of Personal Growth*. You will uncover various definitions of Personal Growth, what impact it has had on people just like you, what's possible when more people integrate Personal Growth into their lives, and what are the key insights and wisdom that some of the greatest minds of our time live by.

First, I acknowledge you for your commitment to Personal Growth. I truly honor and respect you for taking the time to better your life and read this book.

You may be aware of Personal Growth and not convinced it's for you. Maybe you're new to this approach to living and looking to take the next step forward. Maybe you're already passionate about Personal Growth. This book is for everyone interested in living an extraordinary life. It's a multi-purpose Personal Growth guide to assist you on your journey.

I have personally interviewed twenty-five of the most influential leaders in the Personal Growth industry and surveyed forty-four individuals who have made a commitment to Personal Growth.

In this concise yet powerful collection of stories and insights by amazing people, you will learn timeless wisdom. Everyone who reads this book will take away something different: Depending on what you're looking for, you'll find clarity, experience, understanding, inspiration, and ultimately be encouraged to make a difference in your life, in the lives of your loved ones, and in the world. When you continue to integrate the concepts of Personal Growth into your life, you will have the power to produce the results you've only dreamed about—until now.

The book is a compilation of hundreds of years of experience in life and Personal Growth. Instead of reading hundreds of books on Personal Growth, this one volume presents succinctly the stories and concepts you may not have read before and would like to know. Personal Growth is all about learning from ourselves and each other. This book encourages exponential growth and awareness. *The Power of Personal Growth* will save you years of figuring out life on your own.

The Need For Personal Growth

More than ever we are in need of Personal Growth on a global level. We are in dire straits because of a general worldwide lack of knowledge and awareness of what's possible when we create extraordinary lives for ourselves and each other. We can all contribute to the one world community and make the planet a better place. The norm has been people who spread negative news, promote fast food and pharmaceutical concoctions rather than address the *cause* of real life issues.

We have been trained, to varying degrees, to obey authority, work hard, and to speak when called on. The educational system instills an early model for learning that conditions our behavior as adults.

Some of you may be going through life, day-in and day-out, just working hard, watching TV, eating junk food, and falling into bed at night. You may be living on *autopilot* rather than directing your energies and living life to its fullest.

Think about it: You are the producer, director, and actor of the movie called *your life*. To live an outstanding life, which includes doing what you love and being all you can be, you need to be proactive and deliberate on *designing* your destiny.

Today's world demands that powerful people step up and take a stand for what's important. Together we can challenge systems that no longer serve us and create new structures that will be designed more effectively to set us up for success.

The quality of our lives depends on us and how we choose to live. The choices we make ultimately shape our lives and many of us are waking up to this fact. With movies such as *What The Bleep Do We Know!?*™ and *The Secret*, people are becoming aware that there is more to life than what meets the eye. **The Power of Personal Growth** offers you significant awareness and knowledge so you can make empowering choices to positively impact your life.

What societies think and feel affect and determine their environments. In Washington, D.C in 1993 a study was conducted in which 4,000 people (1% of the population) meditated twice daily for 8 weeks; the overall city crime rate dropped 23% during the study.

In the book, *Messages in Water* Dr. M. Emoto studied how words affect the composition of water: When you speak empowering words or think positive thoughts about love, joy, and peace, the water crystallizes into beautifully defined shapes. When you say disempowering words and think negative thoughts about hate, war, and anger, the water forms broken separated crystals. As a matter of fact, our bodies as well as the world contain more than 70% water: Just like in Dr. M Emoto's study, it has been proven that the words we think and speak affect our lives, the world and everything around us.

There was another study done with plants. One plant was spoken to in a loving manner, the second plant was yelled at constantly. After a short time, the first plant thrived while the second withered and died. Words have the power to hurt or heal.

My Personal Growth Journey

My journey began in October, 2004, when I was living an unfulfilled life. I had closed my third business in less than one year. I was fifty pounds overweight, clinically depressed, and was more than $100,000 in debt. All of this didn't happen overnight, it had been building for six years.

Near the end of October, I was introduced to my first Personal Growth seminar, which I speak about in greater detail in chapter two. The four days of the seminar were the most confrontational and liberating moments in my life. I released much of my emotional baggage and picked up many useful tools to begin shaping the life of my dreams. Within weeks after the event, I lost forty pounds, eliminated my depression, and started living a passionate life.

Following that seminar, I wondered why everyone didn't know the benefits of Personal Growth and why it wasn't more readily available. Following that first seminar I decided to dedicate my energies to Personal Growth and to building a company that would raise the global awareness of the power of Personal Growth for billions of people.

The Personal Growth Advocate™

My vision includes a world where Personal Growth is a way of life for everyone. My role models are: Henry Ford (whose wish was that everyone own an automobile), Bill Gates (who wants everyone to own a computer), and Dr. Martin Luther King Jr. (who desired equality for all).

I am the Personal Growth Advocate™ with the sole mission to support people who want to fulfill their potential and live their dreams.

I believe so much in Personal Growth and its power to transform the world that I put everything I have on the line for this book. I borrowed money from family and friends, cashed in my IRA, used the gift money from my wedding, and was even on the verge of bankruptcy. I know in my heart it will make a significant difference as people integrate Personal Growth into their lives.

My wish is that every single person on the planet has access to Personal Growth. I want to share with everyone what's possible when each of us integrates Personal Growth in our daily lives. It has been said that we tap into only a fraction of our potential—Personal Growth is all about becoming aware and allows us to tap into our endless potential.

Your life is waiting and your loved ones and the world are counting on you. I encourage you to read through the chapters and take action: be inspired, get motivated, and revel in the shared wisdom in this small and important book. If I can support you in any way throughout your journey, feel free to connect with me anytime through PersonalGrowth.com.

Lastly, please share with me the impact of this book on your life. Also, be sure to pass on the book to impact the lives of your family, friends, community, and beyond…

Thank you.

"In times of change, learners inherit the earth; while the learned find themselves beautifully equipped to deal with a world that no longer exists."
~ Eric Hoffer

Understanding Personal Growth

I want everyone to be free of constraints and conditioning, whether cultural, environmental or societal. When this happens, people will live with joy, love, gratitude, and abundance. When people engage fully in a Personal Growth journey they experience a new sense of freedom and purpose that they never had before.

Personal Growth is, at its core, about nurturing the growth of an individual. We are *holistic* beings with a mind, body, and spirit. We live in a world where we are increasingly challenged to draw upon our full potential. Personal Growth helps us to rise to the occasion—to become all that we may be and adapt to the lightning-speed changes in society.

Personal Growth and Spiritual growth are very intertwined. As Teilhard de Chardin said, *We are not human beings having a spiritual experience. We are spiritual beings having a human experience.* Is it an innate force that propels us forward to engage in life and everything around us? Some say the force is God, the Universe, the Divine Spirit, or something else. For me, it is the Spiritual that both moves and defines us. Personal Growth is the connection to that innate power, which allows an individual to grow and live life to the fullest.

Many people are not aware or do not understand what Personal Growth is. I believe one of the core reasons is because it is called by so many names. Personal Growth may also be known by: self help, personal development, self-improvement, new age, and many others.

In my opinion, once we choose a name for the concept of the growth of an individual, even more people will understand what's possible for them and the world. I feel that Personal Growth is the best name.

Personal Growth is a solo journey and one you don't have to embark on alone. Even though you take the journey yourself, others are working on their journey as well. When we support each other everyone grows exponentially.

For me, Personal Growth is a way of life – a way of being, thinking, feeling, and acting. It begs the questions: What do you think about during the day? How do you feel most of the time? How proactive are you in life? To what level are you playing in life? Who are you?

We are creatures of habit. Have you been thinking, feeling, or acting in a certain fashion for too long and want to break with old patterns? By fully embracing Personal Growth and taking action to change, you can transform your life and start thinking, feeling, and acting in brand new ways.

Myths About Personal Growth

There are so many myths about Personal Growth. These myths are also part of the reason why more people do not yet know the true power of Personal Growth. Let's take a look at a couple of them so you can see for yourself the value in Personal Growth.

Myth # 1: Personal Growth is only for people who need help.

The truth is that many people find Personal Growth at different points in their lives. Some people are looking for help with a crisis while others are looking to develop skills to improve their lives. Many people work through difficult life situations with Personal Growth techniques. People may explore it, for example, when they want to improve their health, make more money, or enhance their relationships. In my experience, Personal Growth supports people who clearly state their dreams and commit to living life to its fullest potential. Personal Growth is for everyone.

Myth # 2: Personal Growth is a religion or cult.

Unlike a cult, there is no one path or person that you are forced to follow in Personal Growth. You study what you want at your own pace - you choose your own journey. With some religions and cults, you are told what to think, how to act, and what to do. Personal Growth is open and available to everyone regardless of age, race, culture, religion, and any other element of segregation.

Each person explores freely who he wants to be, how he wants to grow and change, what he wants to achieve, and how he plans to get there. In Personal Growth, nobody tells you what you can and should do – it is completely up to you to create your own plan of action. Everything you desire, dream, and want is available to you when you are willing to dedicate yourself to life long learning.

Abraham Lincoln says it best, *If I had eight hours to chop down a tree, I'd spend six hours sharpening my ax.*

How To Read This Book

The Power of Personal Growth explores what Personal Growth is, illustrates its value and demonstrates what's possible for you, your loved ones and the world at large.

The book offers an inside view of the impact Personal Growth has had on the 56 people who contributed to this book. You discover what Personal Growth means to them, the impact it has had on their lives, what they envision is possible for themselves and the world, and wisdom they live by that makes all the difference for them.

The interviews represent collectively hundreds of years of experience of Personal Growth. I'm grateful to those who have opened up and generously shared their journey—the stories offer pearls of insights that you, the reader, may take pleasure in while reading *The Power of Personal Growth*.

There are several ways to read this book. First, you may choose to read the book from cover to cover - starting at the beginning and reading straight through to the end. This will provide you with a great overview of the impact Personal Growth can have on your life.

Second, you may choose to read the book in sections, specific chapters, story topics, or read only what particular individuals have to say. If you prefer to read selectively, you will find an index in the back of the book that will help you navigate the content.

Third, you may opt to read random pages. Have fun with it! Every page is filled with insights and wisdom that will positively impact your life.

I recommend that you explore all the options and allow the insights and lessons in this book to become fully integrated into your life. I also invite you while reading to write down those insights, action items, and a-ha moments at the end of each chapter on the lines provided.

The Power of Personal Growth is a book to re-read throughout your Personal Growth journey. As you grow and evolve, you will continually discover new nuggets of wisdom that speak to you at one point in your life or another.

Turn the page to experience your exponential growth... and enjoy the power of Personal Growth.

1 What is Personal Growth, Anyway?

"The whole point of being alive is to evolve into the complete person you were intended to be."
~ Oprah Winfrey

"The only thing more expensive than education is ignorance."
~ Benjamin Franklin

Everyone defines Personal Growth in his or her own terms. It is amazing how many people refer to it as a journey, while others look at it as an evolution.

In this chapter, a group of individuals and industry leaders have generously shared what Personal Growth means to them. There is so much wisdom in each and every one of their statements—a richness of experience in life that helps us understand who we are and why we are here.

~ George Lodge ~

"Personal Growth is the pursuit of positive activities, experiences, and education: The process expands your consciousness and opens you up to possibilities far beyond your currently perceived limits and boundaries."

~ Kathryn Arnold ~

"…A constant examination of what is and isn't working in your life, and an exploration of new ways of being to achieve a fulfilling life, which is composed of health, wealth, love, and personal self-expression."

~ Matthew Britt ~

"We are alive, and if we aren't growing we are dying. Make sure you're growing! Lifelong learning and striving for growth are the secrets to life."

~ Debbie Hoogestraat ~

"The willingness and ability to look at life situations head on and to make informed choices is empowering. Instead of making decisions based on fear and negative past experiences, everybody can learn new strategies to succeed each day. At the heart of the matter are growth and change."

~ Eric Turiansky ~

"Discovering who we are is a lifelong pursuit. The process embraces the spiritual, emotional, and intellectual aspects of ourselves. It is the journey, not the destination!"

~ Monika Zands. ~

"The study of the self is both an internal and external experience. The gamut of lessons we learn along the way shows us how to break habits and patterns so we expand from what we think is available to us or possible in our lives."

~ Lee Lam ~

"Living more fully means the ability to open yourself up to the possibility that you are capable of more than you are currently doing. It is about recognizing the frustration you feel about where you are in your life, the negative and positive feelings you have about yourself, and knowing that there is more about you that you haven't developed yet."

~ Korby Waters ~

"Personal Growth is the willingness to go through whatever it takes to express yourself. In essence, being uncomfortably comfortable becomes a new way of being—and will give you more juice in your life."

~ *Lew Bronstein* ~

"Learning something new and applying it each and every day gives meaning and purpose to our lives. Growth is the ability to learn how to take any situation either good or bad and get the most out of it, and then share what you've learned from the experience. Making progress in life is about taking responsibility for ourselves and being responsible to others. It is about using past pains as a motivator to embrace future pleasures. In summary it is about our stepping up to the plate of being all we can be and then striving for more!"

~ *Manny Goldman* ~
Author and Founder, PersonalGrowth.com

"Personal Growth encourages proactive learning. Here's a metaphor to describe it: *you can water a plant or wait for it to rain*. Each action or reaction has a very different outcome. When you water a plant, you are proactively providing the resource required for its growth. The same concept applies to your life. You can either create the life of your dreams or settle for what you get.

"Personal Growth is a personal journey about becoming aware, obtaining knowledge, and learning from every situation in life. It is about being grateful, optimistic, and going after what you want.

"There are many ways to experience Personal Growth, such as: attending seminars, reading books, listening to audio programs, watching inspirational movies, having a mentor or coach, spending time with supportive friends, meditating, journaling and especially finding lessons in everyday experiences.

"Personal Growth speeds up the process of taking in and absorbing wisdom fully so you don't have to learn through repeated trial and error. One of the quickest methods to accelerating your Personal Growth is to consider the company you keep: Surround yourself with people who believe in you and will hold you accountable to fulfilling your full potential and living your dreams."

~ Cynthia Kersey ~
Author of *Unstoppable* and *Unstoppable Women*

"To me, Personal Growth is raising your consciousness and getting in touch more deeply with who you really are on an authentic level. Taking responsibility for your life and the results you are creating is the basic entry point of growth.

"To do this we must first understand that how we interpret the events of our lives determines everything; how we feel, how optimistic we are, how we respond to our circumstances, and what we will ultimately create for ourselves. Our thoughts create our life's experience. Once we understand this at a deep level is when Personal Growth can really begin.

"The practice of Personal Growth helps us release limitations as to what's really possible in our lives: It's about shedding illusion and false beliefs that give us the feeling we are separate, not good enough or can't have or be the person we truly desire to be."

~ Jennifer S. Wilkov ~
Best-selling Author of *Dating Your Money,*
Publisher and Book Consultant

"Personal Growth is an opportunity to let go, learn something new, integrate changes into our lives, and live life easily. It is about seeking new information to enhance our life experiences.

"Personal Growth is available to each of us, through a simple conversation with someone where we become aware of how we are thinking and feeling about our lives. Books, audiotapes, live events and teleseminars make it easy to find the information and teachers to support you through thoughtfully designed programs and presentations for any area of interest."

~ Pat Finn ~
CEO, Rubicon Results Institute

"Personal Growth is a combination of what, in the past, we have called self help, self improvement, transformation, and spirituality. It is about taking responsibility for knowing that all 'growth' starts within."

~ David "Avocado" Wolfe ~
Author, Entrepreneur, and Raw Food Expert

"Since the 1900s, Personal Growth has been the science and fine art of personal transformation—the path from caterpillar to butterfly. It is a process of self-mastery that is startlingly simple, yet sophisticated. Personal Growth is activated through stages of discipline practiced daily."

~ T. Harv Eker ~
Author of NY Times #1 Best-seller
Secrets of the Millionaire Mind™

"Very simply stated, work on yourself with the intention of growing yourself. What does that mean? Most people work from the outside—they work on their job, business, marketing, negotiations, finance, money, and even relationships. They work on all kinds of exterior things in their lives.

"Most people don't work on them. What do I mean by 'them'? Personal Growth is working on your mind-set, attitude, characteristics, the way you think and your habits—working from the inside.

"Who are you?

"One of the sayings I use in my course is, 'Fortunately or unfortunately, you take yourself with you wherever you go.' The answers are not outside of you. The answers are you."

~ Robert G. Allen ~
Best-selling Author of *Multiple Streams of Income*

"'Personal Growth': two great words coming together to spell out what it means to become better and better.

"Growth is the result of being able to deal with challenges, struggles, difficulties, barriers, obstacles, and problems. It's the process of becoming human, and growing from the lower self to the higher self."

~ Lin Morel, MA, DSS ~
CEO, Beyond Words Group;
Transformational Women's Groups & Keynotes

"The full embodiment of spiritual expression is, to me, the highest pinnacle of Personal Growth. It is about taking responsibility for your development as a human being. As Teilhard de Chardin said, *'We are spiritual beings having a human experience.'*

"Those who walk the path of Personal Growth are consciously aware that their thoughts and actions affect everyone around them. Native Americans, the Seneca in particular, say that anything you say or do affects seven generations. Personal Growth makes us mindful that we impact the world around us with our words, actions and deeds."

~ Jack Canfield ~
CEO, The Canfield Training Institute;
featured teacher in *The Secret*

"I believe that we're all born with a potential to maximize our lives. If we are conscious about our powers, we can choose to focus on growing ourselves in a number of different ways.

"I teach the 'holistic model,' which says that we are a higher self, a spiritual being incarnated in a physical body with an intellect, emotions, and imagination, intuition and a will. I'm aware of who I am and what I think. I'm aware of what I feel. Who's the 'I'? The 'I' is the center of awareness.

"My higher spiritual self knows that the essence of change is awareness. People can become more focused using their willpower: For example, we talk about using our willpower to set New Year's resolutions and achieve goals.

"As to the intellect, much of the intellect is informed by beliefs, mostly programmed by our parents, grandparents, friends, the community, school, and work. The programming doesn't always know the truth about how the world is and how it works. Instead, we're programmed to have fears about life, relationships, and money.

"It is our responsibility to grow ourselves intellectually: I have read more than 3,000 books, and encourage people to read, attend seminars, and listen to audiotapes to challenge themselves and their beliefs about the world.

"To grow emotionally, we need to know that it's okay to experience the depths of our feelings. Men need to know they can be sad and cry—it won't make them a wuss or a sissy. Women need to know that they can get angry and define boundaries without feeling they are bitchy.

"Many of our feelings are the result of our thoughts about how the world should be. When the world doesn't match up, we feel resentment and anger. I use metaphors for getting angry: You come home and find cow manure in your living room. The first couple times, you just clean it up and get your living room back in shape. Eventually you ask, 'Where's the cow coming from?'

"If you're angry or scared all the time, you can pinpoint and change those thoughts that are producing negative emotions. That's a very important part of Personal Growth.

"People have active imaginations. We need to harness our imagination to serve our goals and align us with our higher self, our life purpose. We can learn to visualize positive outcomes rather than negative outcomes, which are a by-product of worry.

"Visualization is probably the least understood tool. Yet we think visually more than verbally or subauditorily. From research we have learned that we can program our subconscious mind with visualizations because the unconscious mind thinks visually.

"Intuition is knowing what we know without knowing how we know it. Most of us are talked out of trusting our intuition and are instead asked: 'How do you explain that rationally? What's your defense for that? Where are the statistics?'

"When we know we don't trust a person, we know when we shouldn't pursue a business opportunity. We feel it in our gut. For me, when I get a tight feeling in my chest, I know something is not right. If I get an expansive feeling in my chest, I know I can go ahead. And I get goose bumps when something is spiritually clear! If I get a great idea, my body tells me whether it will work. We have to learn the language of our intuition.

"Personal Growth also involves keeping our body healthy, exercising, remaining fit, and learning to love and nurture our body. I make a commitment to get 26 massages a year! Every two weeks, I schedule one to make sure I relax. Yoga and Pilates are excellent for stretching and flexibility. Our heart and lungs need endurance and aerobic exercise, and we need to do strength training for our muscles.

"Personal Growth, including health and nutrition, teaches us to laugh and be light and understand the power of our mind and imagination to trust our intuition and be in alignment with our higher self."

~ *Blair Singer* ~
The Creator of SalesDogs®

"I've been in the Personal Growth industry since 1980. I've taught hundreds of thousands of people, thousands of businesses and worked with some incredibly great masters and gurus.

"My definition of Personal Growth is twofold: there is a natural Personal Growth and a formal Personal Growth. What I mean is the following: Through the course of your life, you grow naturally through trial and error. From all the experiences you have, you grow whether you know it or not. How positive your experiences are and how much you leverage them depends on the second part of Personal Growth, which is the more formal part. This comes from formal education and training: books, audio and video programs, seminars, coaching, and mentors. Both of these formats of Personal Growth are aimed to allow you to win the battle of your own brain. It takes initiative to develop yourself.

"Therefore, I don't see a huge difference between natural Personal Growth and formal Personal Growth. In reality they're one and the same. The development of oneself is an activity and growth is the offshoot. It's like developing real estate. As you develop the property, the property grows in value.

"Whether you like it or not, you're growing: If you go out and stub your toe, you experience Personal Growth. The question is: Are you aware that whatever happens to you is an opportunity to grow and leverage that experience? This is accelerated Personal Growth!

"From my perspective, it really boils down to the battle of the brain. We trademarked the name 'Little Voice Management™,' which is a tool to win the battle of your own brain and be 'at cause' rather than 'at effect'. When you strive to be at cause, you find that you're able to better control the game of life."

~ Alison A. Armstrong ~
CEO and co-founder of PAX Programs Incorporated

"Personal Growth is about personal responsibility.

"An individual can make a difference in life—in the lives of other people, organizations, communities, society, and the world. One individual can do all of that and more.

"The idea that one individual can make a difference in the world still inspires me. Change begins with taking personal responsibility. Any area in which a human being decides to be responsible, not to blame or be blamed, but to voluntarily be responsible for something or someone larger than himself, truly has the power."

~ Les Brown ~
Author of the highly acclaimed and
successful book, *Live Your Dreams*

"Personal Growth, to me, is challenging yourself to find out what makes you who you are. It's always reaching to discover more about yourself through projects, goals and activities you engage in to help bring you to that place."

~ Kim Castle ~
Brand Visioneer, Co-creator BrandU®

"You get involved in Personal Growth to become the fullest expression of who you are and how you relate to the whole. It is an ongoing commitment to be the very best that you can be."

~ Sarah Singer-Nourie ~
Founder, Singer Learning, Inc.

"To me, Personal Growth is about following a personal path that's actively challenging, questioning, and revealing—all for the purpose of tapping into your own potential, realized or not."

~ Raymond Aaron ~
The Nation's Number #1 Success and Investment Coach

"My definition of Personal Growth? It's three words long: 'Address your demons!' The demons are inner turmoil and struggles. We have names for our challenges, such as 'defensiveness,' 'being a victim,' 'being an abuser,' 'talking way too much,' 'being fearful,' or 'feeling ashamed.'

"Whatever your demons are, they normally hold you down, ruin opportunities, and mar your reputation. When you do Personal Growth work, which is difficult work, you get to address your demons, clobber them, and push them on their merry way.

"Personal Growth has been the most profound and wonderful journey of my life."

~ Gary Ryan Blair ~
Best-selling Author and President of The Goals Guy

"Personal Growth is a lifelong pursuit because life is a work in progress. You never totally arrive; there's always some polishing to do, knowledge to gain, and love to deepen."

Conclusion

From each definition in this chapter, you begin to see that Personal Growth is about possibility, focusing on what you want, and living your full potential.

Personal Growth is in the process of being commonly understood and accepted in society. Many of us have been enjoying its value for years, while some of us may be learning about the benefits of Personal Growth for the first time.

As you read on, I ask that you start exploring what Personal Growth means to you as you enjoy making it a way of life.

I encourage you to write down everything that was meaningful to you in this chapter. Make a commitment to yourself to integrate them into your life:

2 How Does Personal Growth Impact Your Life?

*"Every adversity, every failure, every heartache carries
with it the seed of an equal or greater benefit."*
~ Napoleon Hill

*"The secret of life isn't what happens to you, but
what you do with what happens to you."*
~ Dr. Norman Vincent Peale

Personal Growth has the potential to literally transform any area of your life. You have to be willing to look at the area, be open to consider some changes and take action to make the necessary adjustments.

You are about to read stories from extraordinary people who have changed their own and others' lives in surprising ways.

The journeys shared by both individuals and industry leaders in this chapter detail what life was like before they discovered Personal Growth and what their lives are like today as a result of making Personal Growth a way of life for them.

~ *Carolyn Ellis* ~

"I was in my late 20s and had just become a mom. At home on maternity leave, I felt I didn't know who I was anymore. Up until the birth of my child, I measured my success by my paycheck and my influence at work. Looking after an infant at home was foreign to me and I wasn't sure I was doing a very good job at it.

Where was the training for becoming a new mom? I remember looking at my schedule and seeing that only a week before the birth of my child my day was filled with meetings with senior government officials and strategy sessions with staff people. Fast-forward and I was now counting the number of dirty diapers per day. I hadn't realized that my self-worth and value were tied up with people outside myself. One morning while holding my baby daughter in my arms, I embraced the notion of defining for myself my own self-worth. A few months later my sister stayed at my house for a transformational workshop. She kept outrageous hours and it sounded like they were doing a lot of weird stuff in the workshop. She invited me to check it out. My brain said, 'No way! It's too far out, maybe even dangerous.' I came up with all sorts of reasons not to accompany her. But then she said, 'I think you'll learn something about yourself that will make you a better parent.' That was all I needed to hear and I agreed to go. I attended my first Personal Growth workshop almost 15 years ago and it opened a door to discover myself."

~ Karen Walker ~

"Through my journey in Personal Growth, I was able to transcend my old life, get rid of fears, regain my self-esteem, and begin a new life. I had been in a very abusive relationship and once upon a time lived in constant fear. I was unable to function on a daily basis until I realized that my fears and my worries were manufactured by me. Even though my surroundings were what they were, I began to understand that I had the power to filter my emotions, balance my perceptions, and control my responses to even the most negative events in my life. Personal Growth freed me!"

~ Edward Munoz ~

"In 1994 I got out of the Marine Corps after serving four years for my country in the Persian Gulf War. I came back to Brooklyn, New York, to a different war—a family living in poverty. I had a choice to become either the victim or victor of my circumstances. I ended up becoming a victim. My parents had just gone through a bad divorce. My younger brother took it hard and quit high school and would not return to the house for days. No one knew where he was. It seemed that he got in with the wrong crowd for a while. My younger sister slipped into a terrible depression and had serious problems with her boyfriend. My mother was clinically depressed and contemplated suicide. They all looked to me for support and inspiration. Mind you, I was trying to be there for them, but I had ended up collapsing into their negative spiral. I fell into depression, slept 10 to 14 hours a day, and even got a potbelly—a real no-no for a Marine. My standards had always been high, but like I said, I allowed myself to become a victim of circumstance.

"To make matters worse I became a taxi driver in the worst area of Brooklyn and my shift was at night. I was also in school and had to live in challenging conditions where I slept in a sleeping bag because there was little to no heat in the apartment. Imagine taking a shower in those conditions. Life really, really sucked. I even got myself into a lot of bad debt—$30,000 to be exact. UNTIL one day I saw an infomercial with Anthony Robbins. His words had a great impact on me. I decided to buy his book, *Awaken the Giant Within*. After reading it, my life changed. I started reading books by other leaders on Personal Growth, and I began regaining my confidence. For the first time in my life I began thinking like a champion and wanted to be successful. Basically I got my hope back and I felt unstoppable. I got my real estate license and joined a real estate company. Within two years I was a sales manager. My task was to recruit and build a sales team. I started with one agent and ended up managing 25 agents. In the next two years I became a partner. Then we opened a mortgage company. Currently we have a 4,000-square-foot location and are renovating. These quantum leaps would not be possible if I hadn't had a date with destiny: encountering Personal Growth in 1995. What I have learned in my pursuit of success, happiness, and fulfillment is that most people spend their time working harder and harder hoping they will have it all someday. In fact, success is not something you pursue but something you attract by being the best person you can be—with that, success just can't help but fall into your lap!"

~ David Sendroff ~

"In my early teens, I used to hang out with the 'bad kids.' We started smoking pot and getting into all sorts of mischief, as troubled kids do. Somehow, I was drawn to these types of kids. When I got my driver's license at age 16, I began sneaking out of the house in the middle of the night and driving 45 miles to all-night raves in Baltimore. Then I got into much harder drugs, including ecstasy, acid, and crystal meth. I focused on the immediate pleasures and was oblivious to the havoc the drugs were wreaking on my body. To slide by in high school I did the minimum, and at 17 I went to college at Kent State University in Ohio. During the first semester I was caught smoking pot and put on probation. At the end of the semester, I transferred to the University of Maryland. Wherever I went, I found drug users and other distractions to keep me from feeling what was going on inside me.

"One day, I saw an infomercial for an audio program called *Personal Power® II*. I sat and watched the whole thing, and when it ended I bought it. The program was a major wake up call: I began looking at what wasn't working in my life and where I was going. At age 19, during my second year of college in November of 1997, my grandparents were near death and my life began flashing desperately before my eyes. My new year's resolution was to quit drugs. No one believed me. I wrote down all the reasons why I was quitting, including my weakened immune system, lack of motivation and having no true friends who really cared about me. I told my parents about my problem and gave them a copy of my resolution to quit drugs so they could hold me accountable.

"It has been 10 years since I've kicked the habit. One of the hardest things I did was to disassociate with all of my old 'friends' who did drugs—everyone I had known at least smoked pot. A new drug-free friend and roommate and I began working out together, and I gained 20 pounds of muscle. My self-esteem began to soar. In 2001, I attended Anthony Robbins' *Unleash the Power Within*. The seminar had the most profound impact on me. I learned about psychology, communication, relationships, and more. My biggest takeaway was that my old worn-out belief system, which had me convinced that 'I was not intelligent', could now be discarded. Inspired by the fact that Anthony Robbins was reading a book every few days at the time, I began doing the same. I was so moved by Anthony that I attended his *Mastery University®* program and headed to the *Date with Destiny®* seminar a few months later. From the seminars I was able to evaluate and redefine my values and beliefs. The 'What if I fail' syndrome had been driving my life. In the past if there was a remote chance of failure, I wouldn't even try. I wanted to look good. Redefining failure opened up new possibilities for success in my life. I began growing from all of the books I was reading, and I was able to get a nice raise at work. My parents and sister started working out, eating healthy foods, and eventually attending seminars too.

"After looking one day at my notes from Anthony's seminar, I made a list of exactly what I was looking for in a woman. Six months later, I met my soul mate, Joie, and she embodied everything on my list to a T. For our second date, I invited her to Anthony's *Unleash the Power Within* seminar. During Joseph McClendon III's guided visualization, we held hands while we all yelled 'I love you!' In that moment, I grabbed her and we kissed. Later, everybody in the group wrote letters to him or herself, which were mailed to us six months later. In the meantime I proposed to Joie. After we moved in together, the letters finally arrived. It brought tears to her eyes as Joie read that I knew she was the one for me ever since our first date. She had written the same in hers. Now, more than ever, I see the power of writing down goals because we attract what we want in our lives. Personal Growth has been the catalyst for a 180-degree shift in my life and it has had a ripple effect on everyone around me, including my soul mate, Joie."

~ Nancy Brandt ~

"My husband left me when I was seven months pregnant. When he left the country I got stuck with the ruined business. I slipped into being the victim and felt depressed and hopeless. I was barely able to care for my children or go to work. Over the course of three years I became bitter and stuck. I felt that I was dealt a bad set of cards. Then a fabulous, caring friend gave me a ticket to an Anthony Robbins seminar and insisted I needed to go for the kids. Feeling desperate, I went to the seminar while feeling that nothing would help. The seminar helped me redefine a future for myself. I was shown what could be if I only changed my disempowering beliefs and also what would happen if I did not change those beliefs.

"In only two years, I have tripled my income. I am writing a book on relationships and I am dating. I love my children, and they smile a lot more now that I am smiling too. What really matters to me is having a loving family and friends. In this environment I have created a wonderful peer group, which supports my new life and way of thinking. I look forward to the future."

~ Matthew Britt ~

"Life before Personal Growth was rather slow. Life seemed to be something happening to me. I was going through the motions on a daily basis. I was living, but I wasn't alive. Looking back on it, I can say that Personal Growth has absolutely, no question about it, made me a happy person with a mission.

"I discovered Personal Growth through my wife. She introduced me to a book called *The Monk Who Sold His Ferrari*, by Robin Sharma. That book opened my eyes and encouraged me to take my life into my own hands.

"My life since discovering Personal Growth has shifted from one with limits to one of abundance. I am now a full-time student of greatness. I spend my time surrounded by top-quality books, audios, magazines, events, courses, and people. I love my life and share it on a daily basis. I want to add value to the world and Personal Growth allows me to make that a reality."

~ Lew Bronstein ~

"I began my journey in Buffalo, New York, while working in the family business. Although people told me I was good in the business, I always felt there was more to life. After a few frustrating years professionally and personally (failing business, failing marriage, and low self-esteem) I moved to Orlando, Florida, to begin a new life. My entrepreneurial spirit returned, and although I became mildly successful in business I felt that I had no real zest for life. In 1998 my baby girl, Lexi, was born and now I had something to live for.

"At the same time I was 30 pounds overweight and didn't respond well to most challenges. Yet in 2004 I went from being a half-assed student of Personal Growth to being 100 percent engaged in my first Anthony Robbins' *Unleash the Power Within* seminar. When we chose buddies, a girl from three rows away turned and shouted out to me: 'You!' I knew then and there that I was supposed to be a leader. Since the seminar I have completed Anthony Robbins' *Mastery University*®, become a member of his *Leadership Academy*®, and enjoy other self-study audio programs and books. One of my missions in life has become to support others, and I help people find ways to change negatives into positives. No one is a failure as long as he is learning and growing.

"I have become a much more balanced person as a result of Personal Growth. I have gone from being judgmental to being accepting. My business has grown exponentially, and my relationship with my daughter, my family, and my friends has strengthened. I have gone from 215 pounds, with high cholesterol, and feeling tired and worn out to becoming a lean, 185-pound, vibrant, clear-eyed powerhouse who feels phenomenal. Everyone around me senses how alert I have become. To sum it up I feel gratitude for the ability to manage my emotions and help others do the same. My two new mottoes are: 'Live, love, and dream with passion' and 'I am love, light, and strength!'"

~ George Lodge ~

"I was living a life according to the beliefs that I had always been taught from the time I was a child: 'Go to school, get a good job, and work hard until you retire.' You know the litany—we've all absorbed it. The problem was, I felt unfulfilled and unhappy, even though I had a fantastic job, a great place to live, and friends and family who loved me. Something was missing. I didn't know what my mission or purpose was, or how to find one. In my late 20s, one of my friends went to an intensive workshop and it created such a positive effect on his life that I decided to go too. The event was the *Landmark Forum*, and it began my Personal Growth journey. It was my first exposure to a different way of thinking about and looking at life, and I came out of it with new ideas and concepts to help me find my purpose. At the same time, I decided: 'I never want to do an intensive again!' At 39, I thought that I had it all nailed down again. Little did I know what the future had in store for me! Great job, great place to live, friends and family that loved me, and again I felt stuck. I wanted to do more with my life.

"My best friend had been working with Peak Potentials Training for the last year. I could see how he was growing and changing as he worked through their curriculum. I wanted to experience this for myself so I attended their *Millionaire Mind Intensive* program, and I was hooked! I became a *Quantum Leap* member with Peak Potentials and started working on myself. I quit my job to seek a new career using my natural gifts and abilities. Greatness is moving forward exponentially beyond where you ever thought you'd be. At 41, I am still on an active Personal Growth track. Some people say I'm crazy for going to all those seminars. At the same time, they admire the way I look at life and my ability to frame situations in a positive manner. They enjoy my energy, say I'm a pleasure to be around, admire my courage not to pursue a traditional career, and applaud my decision to focus on what I love and follow my heart. My mission now is to inspire people to spread peace, joy, understanding, and healing to all, and thereby make the world a better place—and I'm living proof."

~ Dave Ulloa ~

"Prior to discovering Personal Growth, I was a police officer with the Los Angeles Police Department. As a police officer I experienced many horrible life-threatening and life-altering moments that really desensitized me. I became progressively distant, angry, and numb during the five years on the force. I was drinking a lot with other officers or by myself. I watched a lot of TV to escape the pain and dull the thoughts in my mind. Financially, I was on the verge of bankruptcy. My wife and I made decent money but we did not have the discipline to save.

"A few years back while we were making our New Year's resolutions, my wife and I decided to start meditating because we had heard it was a great way to become more centered. At an event we attended there was a silent auction where you could bid on trips, gifts, products, and services. We bid on a CD series called *Get the Edge®* by Anthony Robbins. Retail price was $200 and the opening bid was $60. We won it! The CDs changed my life. We began going to seminars, including Anthony Robbins' *Mastery University®,* and have invested a large sum in our Personal Growth. Our lives have changed for the better: We are happier, healthier, and much wealthier. As entrepreneurs we have control over our destiny. We see the world in a different light now and are attracting amazing people. Recently we've been blessed to co-author a leadership book with Jim Rohn, Zig Ziglar, and Denis Waitley. We have become life coaches for a few select clients. Personal Growth has completely changed our lives. We believe in it and promote its benefits to anyone who will listen."

~ Venloe Scott ~

"My energy used to be channeled through a spatter gun—it was all over the place. I have always been creative and never afraid of tackling *anything.* I became proficient at digging myself into holes and not being able to climb out. Trouble was, this approach zapped my energy and focus. Life became complicated and small tasks became overwhelming. I was a single mother of two children and ended up with a full-time job that barely paid the bills. I juggled well for many years, but there was no margin for error. I started dropping the balls. No money. No relationship. No time.

"In 1999 I started my Personal Growth journey. I completely redefined my goals and values. I worked on the process everyday and included my children, family, and community.

"In 2007 my family is happy: We are involved with each other, not just ships passing in the night. I aligned my social and financial goals and values with those of my family. I founded a small company, we live on a dream property, and our lifestyle suits us fine. Everyday I work toward my vision, which includes more people in my world than it used to. My life is in harmony and it is conducted with integrity: It flows and is exciting. Even though I am thinking and working on my Personal Growth all the time, it doesn't feel like a chore but a pleasure. I now have all the resources I need to achieve whatever I want. I know that everything I wish for, visualize, and focus on—no matter how intangible at the time—becomes a reality."

~ Paul Gruber ~

"I grew up in a small farming community. At an early age I learned about working hard for a living. My father and all my family told me that I must work hard. My early years were spent toiling away, so I never learned much about Personal Growth. As the years passed, I didn't know the true meaning of happiness. Hard work with no vision or purpose made me feel unhappy and unfulfilled. I felt suicidal, began living recklessly, and got in trouble with the law. At this point I discovered God and decided to start living life differently. I committed to my Personal Growth, and found that the more I learned and grew, the more I wanted to learn and grow. Today I'm a full-time student of Personal Growth. I say full-time because I learn from everything I do—from the time I get up at 4 a.m. and review my vision board until the time I fall asleep at night."

~ Eric Turiansky ~

"My first exposure to Personal Growth was when I found my dad's copy of Anthony Robbins' *Personal Power® II*. As a teenager, the audio program enlightened me; I understood that people of all ages could be on a path of Personal Growth. Up until this time, I had felt pretty unmotivated, unsure of my path in life, and believed something was wrong with me. After studying Personal Growth, I know that developing a path is a lifelong process. There are no quick fixes to daily problems, but Personal Growth certainly provides a powerful catalyst to change the way we perceive ourselves and the world around us."

~ Dave Razo ~

"As a teenager I was lost, without direction, and felt miserable. I knew I had potential, but never could seem to develop it. Then I bought a Personal Growth book that explained to me that my thoughts actually produced the life I was living. Since that time I have been a long-term believer in the power of Personal Growth. I know that my inner world, my thoughts, beliefs, and values manifest in the outer world and create my destiny. Over the past 30 years I have traveled the world as an Air Force pilot, have completed three master's degrees, and most important, I have a loving wife and family. I have recently embarked upon a new journey: my own company, which invests and trades in stocks and options. The principles of Personal Growth are ever present in my life."

~ Judith Akins ~

"When I was 16 I became pregnant. My mother bought me a one-way ticket to Sydney, Australia, and told me not to bring my problems home to her. In 1970 there were no benefits for single mothers. I put my baby up for adoption and got on with my life. When my son turned 18 we connected and became really close. In 2000 he attended a Personal Growth seminar at which I was on the Logistic Team. During the seminar, he revisited the circumstances around his birth and shared them with me. Memories of it came flooding back to me and I began remembering what he and his birth were like for me. For 35 years I protected myself from feeling the pain of giving up my baby. Since then I have allowed the archetype of the lover to step forward and replaced the image of the warrior. The experience has changed my life."

~ Manny Goldman ~
Author and Founder, PersonalGrowth.com

"In a short period of time, I have experienced many life lessons. Prior to Personal Growth, I learned the hard way. Looking back, I wouldn't change anything because those lessons have shaped who I am today.

"I was a troubled kid from age 3, and my difficulties continued straight through my early 20s. I have been arrested for fighting, for selling drugs, and twice for driving while intoxicated (DWI). Throughout my childhood, I struggled to understand who I was, and constantly found myself turning to the wrong crowd for approval.

"I was clueless about managing my emotions: I was depressed for many years and was on and off medication for this condition. My relationships were up and down. I had failed not only at several relationships but also in several businesses. Right before I found Personal Growth, I hit rock bottom: I weighed 245 pounds, was clinically depressed for more than 10 years, and had failed in a third business within the year. When I closed down the last business, I was in debt for more than $100,000 and felt completely lost and confused about what to do with my life.

"As fate would have it a postcard came in the mail: Anthony Robbins was having his *Unleash the Power Within* weekend close to my house. I felt this was just the solution I needed and asked several people to accompany me. After finding little interest in my invitation, a friend and former client finally volunteered to come with me to the event.

"The weekend was extraordinary and became a turning point in my life: I gained greater awareness, insight, and wisdom to begin exploring what was possible for my life. In a short time, I lost 40lbs, got rid of my depression, became engaged to the woman of my dreams, moved to California, and found purpose in my life. Over the last three years, I have dedicated myself to my own Personal Growth and living my life purpose: to raise the global awareness of the power of Personal Growth for billions of people. If they choose, they too can make it a way of life.

"One of the greatest gifts I have received during my Personal Growth journey has been seeing the impact on my family and friends. Many of them have embraced Personal Growth in their own way. I've seen amazing results in their lives. I am extremely grateful to see the ripple effect in my life from my willingness to share it with them.

"As student and leader, I look at Personal Growth today as integral to my life as breathing, eating, and sleeping. I have attended and volunteered at more than 50 seminars, read dozens of books on the subject, and listened to countless audio programs. Everyday I learn from people from all walks of life who share a similar path—people who want to examine life and their actions, have a thirst for knowledge, apply what they learn, and create positive experiences in their and others' lives.

"I visualize what it is that I want and the steps I am going to take to get there: I define, redefine, and refine my goals and the steps to reach them. I enjoy meeting amazing people who are invested in their own Personal Growth because they care about being the best he can be.

"Personal Growth is about being proactive rather than reactive, growing and evolving, and living life to the fullest. My passion is to share the power of Personal Growth with everyone around the globe."

~ Pat Finn ~
CEO, Rubicon Results Institute

"I was a broke part-time TV weatherman in San Francisco when I did the *Landmark Forum* in 1989. That weekend I was able to transform my paradigm around money and success. Within 6 months I was hosting the first of several national TV shows and bought the first of several businesses. ...Anything is possible!"

~ Les Brown ~
Author of the highly acclaimed and
successful book, *Live Your Dreams*

"I was born with my twin brother in an abandoned building of a poor section called Liberty City in Miami, Florida. We were adopted at six weeks.

"In fifth grade I was identified as Educable Mentally Retarded (EMR) and was put back a grade. I was considered EMR throughout high school too, and I didn't go to college. My mother was a domestic worker in Miami. Fortunately for me, I had a job too. I kept Mr. Sadirski's office spotless and I shined his shoes.

"They say coincidence is God's way of staying anonymous. When I cleaned Mr. Sadirski's office, he would listen to Dr. Norman Vincent Peale, *The Power of Positive Thinking*, and Earl Nightingale, *Lead the Field* and *The Strangest Secret in the World*. Being exposed to those messages changed my life: It challenged me to look beyond making up beds, cleaning homes, cleaning toilets, scrubbing floors, and raking yards.

"An 11th grade teacher, Mr. Leroy Washington, who happened to be a disciple of Dr. Norman Vincent Peale, challenged me one day in class. I responded to his request: 'Sir, I can't do that.' He said, 'Why not?' I responded, 'Because I'm not one of your students.' He said, 'It doesn't matter. Follow my directions anyhow.'

"I replied, 'Sir, I can't do what you're asking.' The other students began to laugh. Finally, one of them said to the teacher, 'He's Lesley, that's not Wesley. Wesley is the smart twin. He's the dumb twin.'

"The teacher came from behind his desk and examined me while the students were laughing. He said to me: *'Someone's opinion of you does not have to become your reality.'*

"On one hand, I was humiliated. On the other hand, I was liberated because he looked at me with the eyes of Goethe, who said, *'Look at a man the way that he is, he only becomes worse. But look at him as if he were what he could be and he becomes what he should be.'*

"The same teacher said, 'Mr. Brown, work on yourself. *'Be ye not conformed to this world, but be ye transformed by the renewing of your mind.'* People don't live life as it is. They live life as they are.

"Working on my mind became my magnificent obsession. And as my teacher also instructed: *'Develop your communication skills, because once you open your mouth, you tell the world who you are.'*

"It is said that a career is something that you love so much that you'd do it for nothing, but you do it so well that people pay you. I began to get requests from churches, clubs, organizations, and corporations to speak. As a result of my joining the National

Speakers Association, which gave me a larger platform to be seen and heard by people from across the country and around the world, I was able to secure a spot on PBS producing specials. One was called *You Deserve*, which got me national recognition.

"Toastmasters International conducted a poll to find out who were the top five speakers in the world. At the time, General Norman Schwarzkopf, Robert Schuller, Barbara Walters, Paul Hobby, and I were selected. When I received that acknowledgement and the president of Toastmasters said I received more votes than all of the others combined, I was very proud of my accomplishment. The level of recognition and honors I received promised a new beginning—not only the Golden Gavel award from Toastmasters International, but also the CPAE Award from the National Speakers Association, the largest professional speaker's organization. Their award is for top speakers, whose names are entered in the Speakers Hall of Fame.

"My greatest asset to the industry is not as a speaker. There are many great speakers. My greatest asset is as a coach. I teach people how to find their voice, how to create value, and how to seize special moments and opportunities.

"My favorite book says, *'Faith comes by hearing and hearing and hearing.'*"

~ Sarah Singer-Nourie ~
Founder, Singer Learning, Inc.

"I was 10 years old, hated school, and was labeled as a kid with an attitude problem. I had conflicts with teachers and spent a lot of time in the hallway. It was not because I didn't like learning. It was quite the opposite. I loved investigating: taking things apart and putting them back together. I was very curious for my age and was reading before I was supposed to. Yet early on, school felt restrictive.

"I've always listened to a little voice in my head, which sometimes is and sometimes isn't in alignment with what's going on around me. The voice usually asks two questions: 'What's in it for me?' and 'Is there a better way than this?'

"The 'What's in it for me?' question came out of my mouth a lot of the time. I would raise my hand in class and say things like, 'So what does this have to do with real life? Where can we actually use this outside of school? Isn't there some other way we could be doing this that's a little more fun?' As you can imagine, my teachers didn't want to get into that conversation with me. I learned that the most fun I was going to have in classes was seeing how quickly I could get myself kicked out of a class.

"Looking back on it, I was not a traditional learner - I was a very kinesthetic, concrete-random, outside-the-box learner. My learning style didn't fit with conventional education.

"My oldest brother, Blair Singer, who is also active in the Personal Growth industry, said: 'There's this program you need to go check out. It's called: *SuperCamp®*. It's 10 days out of your life. You'll go and then you'll want to come back to school.'

"I told him, 'Forget it! What is it, some summer school? There's no way.' And he said, 'You need to go do this thing. It's going to change the way you look at not just school, but the way you look at yourself.' I was a sophomore in high school and said, 'There's no way.' He explained that it had to do with accelerated learning. That year the one school project I initiated was a paper I wrote, researching accelerated learning—right brain/left brain learning. I suddenly agreed, 'Okay. I'll check out this thing called: *SuperCamp®*.' So I did.

"I went, and it was a major shift for me. Those 10 days turned me into a different person in terms of learning, leadership, and tapping into my own potential. Then the big light bulb came on for me: I wasn't crazy. I spent so many years wondering, 'What's wrong with me? I'm not buying into the system that everyone else thinks is so great.' There was nothing wrong with me—I just learned in a different way than my teachers had been trying to teach me.

"At the time, *SuperCamp®* was like an Outward Bound–type of physical-kinesthetic learning program, which brought in the best of the best in the field of accelerated learning and Personal

Growth. Started and run by Eric Jensen and Bobbi DePorter, Anthony Robbins was a major part of the program, as well as people like Scott Bornstein.

"*SuperCamp®* shifted my thinking from being the troublemaker in school to the kid who was holding workshops for teachers after school. I shared with them how they could teach in a way that tapped into how kids learn and how to make education more fun.

"I decided to become an educator because I wanted to change the system. I wanted to create a method of teaching where kids could be who they were, learn the way they learn best, and be challenged by programs based on relationships, accelerated learning, teams, and fun.

"This was my introduction into the world of Personal Growth: *SuperCamp®* taught me how to approach Personal Growth and accelerated learning.

"In the way I run my workshops today, what people remember, in addition to the content, is the way that I deliver it. It's a fusion of accelerated learning, high energy and high visual/auditory/kinesthetic *state* changes. It's a lot of fun.

"My vision is: If we can make positive changes in the way educators teach and in the school environment, kids' futures will change for the better. Kids will come out of the system having gotten both content and process, and establish a foundation for lifelong learning.

"Today I split my time between my own Personal Growth leadership programs, coaching, and doing work in schools where the heart of learning lies."

~ *Jennifer S. Wilkov* ~
Best-selling Author of *Dating Your Money*,
Publisher and Book Consultant

"I was the second child to divorced parents, and married to a man who had no spiritual interests. My marriage felt more like a companionship than an intimate relationship: Romance was not the norm. My husband and I soon began growing in different directions: We increasingly developed different interests and lifestyles that were no longer working well together. We finally agreed to divorce."

"I started learning more about myself through Personal Growth programs. Because of the work in Personal Growth, my ex-husband and I were able to move through the divorce with respect for each other. I felt blessed that we were able to communicate openly throughout the break up as compared to the uncomfortable experiences I felt during my parents' divorce years earlier.

"In addition, I had been living for 25 years with Crohn's disease, a debilitating health condition that affects the digestive system. I experienced countless numbers of times when I would double over in pain with everyone surrounding me, wanting to help and support me but not knowing what to do—feeling helpless like me. Because of the illness, I had multiple emergency room visits, surgeries, and hospital stays. After my second surgery, I returned home and promised myself I would find a way to stop the disease, even though it had been clearly stated that there was no cure. I made up my mind to get off every drug therapy and begin a journey toward excellent health. After six months of researching alternative methods for treating the condition, I was able to miraculously eliminate all drug treatments.

"My first experience with Personal Growth came from a week-long program in Northern California. In the summer of 2001 I met my beloved sensei, H. F. Ito, through the American School for Japanese Arts. I found a martial art in the program that was both holistic and focused on the synergistic development of the body, mind, and spirit.

"As one of the founding members of the art of Shintaido, Ito Sensei taught that the practice was rooted in learning about yourself and your relationship with nature, other people, and the world around you. Through body movement, Shintaido teaches that the body is a message to the Universe. It's about a moment—each moment—in which you have only one opportunity to express your fullest and greatest self. Ito Sensei and I agreed to become master and student. One day, he explained something about commitment to me that was so clear: 'I can only show you the movements and the way to practice. You have to do it yourself in order for it to work and for you to learn from it. Learn from your commitment to the practice and the value of experiencing the movement yourself.'

"The following year as I continued to seek ways to support my recovery from many years of suffering from Crohn's disease, I attended a weekend seminar program with Anthony Robbins. As the saying goes, my life has never been the same again. The program opened my eyes to a whole new way of approaching my life, aspirations, and dreams. I became determined to travel and to live my life to the fullest. The program was the beginning of a great quantum leap in my personal evolution.

"Traveling to the programs I signed up for was important because when I had Crohn's disease I believed that traveling abroad was too difficult for me. Breaking through my limiting beliefs was a milestone and I traveled to Australia and Fiji for programs that truly transformed my perspective on life.

"I became hooked on Personal Growth and found that the more programs I took, the more accelerated growth and learning resulted in my life. I would attend a program, take away three key points, review my notes, and start implementing right away. I got so adept at the process that one year, I took 10 programs—averaging almost one a month!

"Sharing insight, knowledge, and wisdom that I learn through Shintaido and talking with others about their lives and interests are the most important activities I enjoy. By understanding our commitments and desires, we are able to support each other's goals and dreams.

"Calling out my goals has made so much happen in my life: from beating Crohn's disease and traveling abroad to writing and publishing my first book in 90 days. My mentors and teachers also helped me to realize one of the most rewarding goals in life: I am now a best-selling award-winning author, book consultant, and publisher. Publishing and writing are so meaningful for me. I have a joy and passion for publishing and assisting people with sharing their stories. Teaching others how to write and produce a book in 90 days is thrilling. To see the spark in their eyes and a knowing that 'yes! they can do it!' are incredible gifts I feel blessed to share with them.

"When I meet people interested in publishing their own books— *I'm on fire*. I show budding writers how to produce books using Earth-friendly environmentally sound practices and resources. Proactively educating writers that they have a choice of working with large companies or an option to publish their work on their own is very fulfilling. Showing authors how to work with their book as a business to properly market their message is so rewarding. When I write, publish, or teach my well-known workshop called *Your Book Is Your Hook*™, I feel I am able to share the God-given gifts I have been blessed with.

"By calling out my dream and sharing it with a network of friends, family, and colleagues, I have discovered the most enjoyable and passionate experience in my life today."

~ Robert G. Allen ~
Best-selling Author of *Multiple Streams of Income*

"I can't remember a time when I didn't want to become a better person. I can remember all the challenges and periods of growth in my life.

"There have been many devastating periods in my life, where I experienced a lack of awareness or lack of discipline and I made mistakes, stumbled, fell, and had to learn hard lessons.

"The biggest lesson for me was making a lot of money from my first book and then losing it all because I didn't listen to my intuition. I went through bankruptcy and lost everything. I was at the bottom with nothing. In retrospect it's easy to laugh about, but at the time it was devastating. I felt worthlessness, stupid, and guilty. Beneath worthlessness, lack of self-esteem, guilt, and failure, I learned that there's something else—deep inner resources and a profound sense of personal worth.

"Inner strength exists regardless of external failure, challenges, fears, disappointments, struggles, or low self-esteem. Beneath low self-esteem is your inner wealth. At the bottom of severe financial collapse, I discovered a connection to a Higher Power who loved me, and wanted me to grow, learn, and become just like Him.

"I had a very profound spiritual experience as a result of prayer. I went from a sense of complete financial, personal, and emo-tional devastation to feeling a sweet, peaceful, indescribable love. I realized I was loved regardless of my mistakes—a love that I can hardly express in words. The weight of guilt lifted and I felt lighter and more able to handle the pressures and burdens that I had placed on myself. Regardless of how low I had fallen, I could dig myself out of the hole. I surrendered to my situation and trusted that a Higher Power would show me the way out.

"I had a purpose and destiny in life.

"It took almost 10 years until the debts were all paid off and bankruptcy was behind me. I remember how wonderful it was to write that final check: it was to the IRS for $500,000. To write that check was a very difficult decision because it meant we were broke again.

"It was a profoundly liberating experience.

"Those 10 years of financial collapse were part of my Personal Growth. They meant I had to go back to zero and build a more solid foundation of truth, not a foundation of lies.

"Belief has the word 'lie' in the middle of it and most people's beliefs are lies. My belief about wealth was a lie. My belief about what I could do in life was a lie. My belief about whether I was worthy enough to create a destiny for myself was a lie. I felt I was not worthy of creating wealth. That Heavenly Father didn't love me. All that was a lie.

"Losing everything meant I had nothing left but truth. I could begin anew and build on a foundation of strength and truth.

"There is a Higher Power who loves us and wants us to grow, learn, struggle, and expand. We need to give Him more credit and to involve the Higher Power in our decisions. We need to be part of the Higher Power's team.

"It's better to work toward building a better world. I want to teach people how to have a better life and to have it quicker and less expensively."

~ *Blair Singer* ~
The Creator of SalesDogs®

"What's compelling about my story is that it's not very compelling. Sometimes people go to a Personal Growth program and the speaker talks about all the misery and obstacles they overcame. You walk away thinking, 'Geez, do I have to go through a mountain of misery in order to have enlightenment?' The answer is no.

"My life was pretty ordinary and like many, I wanted more. When I started my journey I had just gone through a painful divorce. Some really great people introduced me to Personal Growth.

"At the time I had a surf shop in Waikiki, Hawaii. A 6' 3" Japanese guy walked into my surf shop, and tried to get me to buy some Velcro nylon wallets. It was Robert Kiyosaki. I told him, 'These guys are surfers. They have no money. What would they need a wallet for?' I was trying to make a joke that didn't go over too well. We've been friends and business partners ever since. He is one of those individuals who introduced me to the world of Personal Growth training.

"Before the surf shop I was financially at the top of my game, working in sales for the Unisys Corporation. I had always been one of those kids who wanted something more. Fast forward to the infamous surf shop meeting: Robert and I both figured that the more we could work on ourselves, the richer we would become. That was the idea. Admittedly, it was purely wealth motivated in the beginning.

"We went through great programs and had great mentors, like Marshall Thurber, who started the *Money & You* program. That was my first real adventure in Personal Growth.

"At one point, I realized that all the money I had made and lost and all of the relationships that had worked and not worked, had one thing in common: me. 'No kidding, you idiot!' But it was a major moment for me: I realized the final frontier was between my right ear and my left ear. As a result, I've spent literally hundreds of thousands of dollars over the years on Personal Growth for myself.

"If you've been to any of my programs, you know I've got a *Little Voice Management*™ CD. It is a compilation of Little Voice Management™ techniques I've learned from my best masters and mentors. I tell people it's a $500,000 CD because that's what I've easily spent just in the last eight years on Personal Growth for myself. It never ends. It never stops.

"It's a way of life. Everything that I do and experience, I wonder, 'How did I make that happen? How do I master the ability to control my environment? And ultimately how can I control that little voice in my brain?'

"The more I process my thoughts, the better my relationships get, the more money we make, and the bigger our business becomes. In addition, my relationships at home with my wife and kids get better along with my health.

"Personal Growth is a way of thinking and being. It's the way we operate our business too: Everybody who comes into our worldwide franchise is required to do Personal Growth training on a continual basis."

~David "Avocado" Wolfe ~
Author, Entrepreneur, and Raw Food Expert

"At 14, during a 10-day summer camp program, I was exposed to the science of Personal Growth. From that point on, I became intimately involved with Personal Growth books, audiotapes, videotapes, seminars, and more.

"I discovered natural foods when I went to college at UC Santa Barbara. I had a girlfriend who first took me into an organic food store.

"I began to realize that certain foods didn't agree with me. The main things were dairy products—cheese, milk, and eggs. I proceeded to cut them all out of my diet. I found that years and years of ear and chronic sinus trouble literally disappeared. I discovered later that ear infections, especially the production of excessive earwax, are the number one response to food allergies.

"Personal Growth has been the single greatest tool box for my self-mastery. The wisdom I have applied from my Personal Growth experiences has deeply affected my relationships, health, nutrition, brainpower, intuition, financial destiny, business skills, philanthropic pursuits, and spiritual life."

~ John Alexandrov ~
Author, Creator of The Money Chi Dotcom

"I found Personal Growth because of some of the challenges I experienced at an early age in my life.

"In my mid-20s I was a very successful businessperson: I had my own law firm and real estate appraisal company. I had all the things in life that somebody would want: a family, my own home, vacation homes, and fancy cars.

"Life was on cruise control.

"I started reading my own press clippings: People were patting me on the back, telling me how well I was doing and how my businesses were so great, etc.

"I took my eye off the ball.

"One day I found out, however, that I was $500,000 in debt. My bank called to say that they were canceling my line of credit; they were going to put me out of business. I went home that night and did a lot of soul searching. I went into my children's rooms and watched them sleep. My children—so innocent, trusting, and vulnerable—made me weep.

"I wondered, 'What have I done? I have this beautiful family. I have this wonderful business. I have everything in life. I can't just let it all slip away because of my own ego.'

"I decided to commit to do whatever I could to turn my business around, even though the bank called my line of credit and the IRS was looking for money from me. I remember driving to my office the next day, looking at Wachusett Mountain, a stunning mountain range in the area where I live, and thinking: 'I will go to the office and do whatever I can to be the best I can be today.'

"As I was looking at the mountain these words came out of my mouth: 'You can take away everything from me. You can take away my home. You can take away my cars. You can take away my businesses. You can even take away my family, but you're not going to take away my self-respect, my dignity, and my ability to be as good as I can possibly be in life.' This became my affirmation. From that day forward, I just stayed committed to doing the best that I could do every single day.

"The story that I just told took place in 1996 and 1997; around the time I was introduced to Personal Growth via a cold call. I was invited to join a coaching class and have been a student for about 10 years.

"In terms of my being a leader, I've watched other people closely in the Personal Growth industry. I've taken a look at what they do, how they do it and why some people succeed and others do not.

"I've chosen some people to become role models for me, even though they're not aware of it. I've emulated what they do in the industry because I admire them."

~ Kim Castle ~
Brand Visioneer, Co-creator BrandU®

"I grew up in a household with a young single mom. We were poor, lived on food stamps, and moved sometimes twice a year. Even though I was young, I knew the welfare we received encouraged dependency. While there was love in my family, there was a lot of anger, instability, drugs, abuse, and victimhood.

"I knew that there was more to life than what I was being shown by my immediate family. I set my goals really high, put myself through college, and now I have a life filled with love, joy, and power. The power to change your life comes from taking personal responsibility and making choices to make sure your dreams come true.

"People usually assume that I went through a lot of therapy to be so balanced and joyful today. The truth is that my equilibrium comes from many sources of Personal Growth, from reading a lot of books, meditation and even fortune cookies from way back when Confucius wrote them."

~ Lin Morel, MA, DSS ~
CEO, Beyond Words Group;
Transformational Women's Groups & Keynotes

"My journey includes going from victim to victor. In the beginning I was the classic victim and didn't have a clue about personal responsibility. Life was not easy.

"I got involved in Personal Growth the same way a lot of people do: I fell into it. In the 60s, my younger sister wanted to take judo and I became her chaperone. I went onto become a fifth degree black belt and nationally ranked karate champion.

"...We grew up in a dysfunctional family. However, I don't really believe there is such a thing as a functional family—maybe a fun-tional family. We were just an average American family with the usual issues and challenges. At 17, I left home and worked my way through college.

"Before my journey into Personal Growth, I would be classified as the victim. I used to worry about being picked on, not being good enough, being too chubby, or nobody liking me. When I began doing martial arts, I learned that I was responsible for everything. Engaging in a competition or a randori (sparring) encourages you to reflect on the outcome. Through the practice I began understanding that the outcome had a great deal to do with being in control of my responses and myself.

"Before martial arts was in my life I didn't have a lot of fun or experience joy. After my involvement in martial arts, I discovered whatever I decided to do could be done simply because I decided it. I learned to set goals whether it was to become a black belt or start out accomplishing smaller goals: to become a yellow belt, then green belt, blue belt, brown belt, and finally a black belt. I stuck with mini-goals, which allowed me to progress slowly but surely. And the universe provided me with plenty of feedback.

"My journey as a student consisted of finding people who knew more than me. Taking advice was a stepping-stone for me: I always wanted to check things out for myself. When my teacher guided me in martial arts, I would follow the instruction. If it didn't work out for me, I'd adjust something a little bit and then the technique would work.

"Early on I understood that learning took place through questioning and the desire to move ahead, familiar concepts to Personal Growth. Moving into a leadership position, beginning with the martial arts, I found that mastery is a very humbling position. For example, when I got my black belt and started teaching, I was immensely humbled by the questions that my students would ask. Inadvertently, they pushed me to think on my feet and deepen my own relationship with my practice so I could better articulate the experience for them.

"The distinction between student and teacher is very amorphous. A wise saying is: *'When the student is ready, the teacher appears.*

When the teacher is ready, the student appears.' I believe that we're all leaders in various aspects of our lives. Some people have just a bit more experience than others. I always look to people who are a couple of steps ahead of me. I've always been drawn to people who excel in the very thing I want to learn. At the same time, everyone is my teacher—including a janitor and the homeless person on the street. Everyone is a mirror image of me. That's what I've learned in my 40-something years of Personal Growth."

~ Bill Bartmann ~
President, Bill Bartmann Enterprises

"One of the more compelling stories of my background is when I was 17 years old and my then girlfriend, who is now my wife, was 14. She was smart enough then to show me that unless I quit speaking negatively about myself, I would never grow or progress. She helped me move forward. That was 45 years ago, then people didn't use the terms 'negative' or 'positive affirmations.'

"The old Chinese saying *'May you live in interesting times'* applies to me: I've had an interesting life. I have gone from living in poverty to becoming the 25th-wealthiest person in America. I've gone from being a 14-year-old runaway to becoming a lawyer and having Harvard Business School do a case study on one of my management techniques. I've gone from a being a teenage alcoholic to being named National Entrepreneur of the Year. I've gone from being a high school dropout to being awarded the American Academy of Achievements' Golden Plate Award. I was a member of a street gang when I was a kid, and now I have a permanent home in the Smithsonian. I've also gone from being $1 million in the hole to over $1 billion in the black.

"To say that Personal Growth has helped me would be the grandest understatement of all times.

"From childhood to early adulthood, I was running in the wrong direction at breakneck speed. I was on a collision course for either a meeting with death or a life in prison. Those were the two choices in front of me. I was able to find a way to Personal Growth and my life transformed. As a teen, I started reading the age-old classic, Napoleon Hill's *Think and Grow Rich*, which is one of the seminal works in the industry.

"Another one of his books has become my bible, it's called *The Laws of Success*, and I continue to read and apply it. It was written 40-plus years ago and remains an ageless classic—the knowledge Napoleon Hill shared back then is still relevant today.

"David Schwartz's *The Magic of Thinking Big* also opened up my brain to thinking for the very first time that we are capable of accomplishing feats that we all thought were impossible.

"I experienced an amazing transformation in my life after reading those books.

"Now I give my own seminars. I teach people what I've learned along the way. I don't think I will ever compare to anybody like Napoleon Hill, David Schwartz or Maxwell Maltz, who wrote *Psycho-Cybernetics*. But in a very humble way, I'm pleased that I'm able to contribute to the cause."

~ *T. Harv Eker* ~
Author of NY Times #1 Best-seller
Secrets of the Millionaire Mind™

"Although we didn't have a lot of money, I didn't have an unhappy childhood. My parents were very loving, however, my dad was very critical and hard on me because of his childhood.

"I wanted to be successful from an early age. When I was 14, 15, or 16 years old I read books like Napoleon Hill's *Think and Grow Rich* and books by Norman Vincent Peale.

"I wasn't getting along with my dad and I was working with him. I took a course called *Mind Power* by John Kehoe. These studies taught me that my thoughts are forces for change. When I was 20, John Kehoe's work taught me about the Law of Attraction. I learned that I could control my own destiny.

"I went from being fairly unhappy, very critical of myself, and not very confident to being very confident. I certainly had my own issues, and I definitely felt like I could control my own destiny.

"One of the lessons I teach in my courses is the difference between how rich people and poor people think. Rich people believe, 'I create my life,' and poor people believe, 'Life is something that happens to me.' This is a huge distinction.

"In fact, rich or poor, we create our reality—today, tomorrow, and every day after that. If things look like they are simply happening to me I can question, 'Gee, how did I create that?' I'm not saying this as a victim, but I'm just saying: 'What's my part in all this?'"

~ *Sarano Kelly* ~
Founder, The Game, and Author,
The Game—Win Your Life in 90 Days

"Much like everyone else, I grew up in a world that was full of projection and blame. I grew up three blocks from Mike Tyson and our neighborhood had the single highest murder rate in the country. By the time I was 16 years old, 50% of the kids that I grew up with were dead. Those who weren't dead went to jail. I am probably the only person from that neighborhood who didn't wind up with prison sentences.

"Growing up, I had a sense of my calling or purpose, which made me curious, open, and willing to consider that I could learn from any person or situation.

"My dad, who had to work two jobs, was illiterate, so later in life he went to school to learn to read and write. He also had a severe medical problem. While I didn't spend all that much time with him, my dad was always there.

"My dad was full of wisdom and shared three pivotal lessons with me. He forced me to take a good hard look at myself. I remember from childhood that he would always say: 'Look in general at what other people do, read, and what they watch. Don't do that.'

I used to sleep until all hours of the day. I'll never forget the time that my dad told me: 'If you get up when everybody else gets up, then the best that you can expect is what everybody else does.' He also said, 'Always play with people better than yourself.'

"At 16 I went to an Ivy League school where everyone else was rich and I was very poor. I became obsessed with material success. I graduated college at 20 and went straight to work on Wall Street. My very first year on Wall Street, I earned, at 23, almost a half million dollars. I achieved a high level of material success at a very young age even though I came from an economically challenged background.

"At the end of that prosperous year, there was a tragedy: four children in my family died in a fire. When I got the call that the kids were dead, I immediately felt both pain and anger—a lot of anger, specifically, toward God... It was very cold the day I drove to the funeral. I'll never forget the thoughts and feelings I had while standing over my cousin's grave. From childhood, my cousin had been an evangelist. She had attended Oral Roberts University and was going to be a true leader in the religious community.

"I had to deal with a paradox: my cousin was dead at 24 and she had never harmed another human being. She had done everything she could to make a difference in other people's lives.

"On the other hand, I was a very arrogant, self-righteous, pretentious, and insecure child, and here I was alive. My life had been spared. I could have easily been there when the four kids died in the fire. I asked myself, 'Why was I here? Was I spared because my life had a purpose?'

"Rather than waiting for my purpose to surface, I created a purpose for myself. My purpose became to help every human being gain access to their full potential. I started with myself. I continued to achieve material success, but it really came from my own Personal Growth.

"In a short period of time while continuing to work on myself, a member of the CIA mentored and trained me. I was responsible for training psychiatrists and psychologists in Advanced Communication Skills. When New York City wanted to train its police in Verbal Judo, I was asked to think about taking on the assignment.

"At 25, I joined the oldest and largest communications training company in the country and became, within four years, the single most successful producer in the history of that company and one of the most successful people in the industry—but the success was no longer just monetary.

"I was changing people's lives. I was giving them access to their full potential. This led me to becoming a media skills coach to the White House. From there, I became the primary coach on Wall Street: I am the only African American motivational speaker and coach to the financial services community on Wall Street.

"My achievements are born out of my father's advice and my early experiences growing up in difficult circumstances. The real trigger, however, was the shock from the death of the kids, which forced me to become more reflective. I had tried to blame the death on God, but it just didn't work. I ended up having to ask myself, 'If this is a lesson, what can I learn?' That's what keeps me going."

~ Cynthia Kersey ~
Author of *Unstoppable* and *Unstoppable Women*

"I started understanding personal responsibility for the first time early on in my marriage. While married in my early 20s, I remembered thinking, 'If my husband would be *more 'X'*: more supportive, work out with me, educate himself, learn about investing... *then*, we'd be happier and more successful, etc. I truly was waiting for him to change with the hopes that I could then get what I really wanted.

"I quickly realized that if I waited for him or anyone else to change, I might be waiting for a long time.

"I finally understood that if I wanted to make any changes in my life, it was really up to me to make it happen. That was the beginning of a whole new path for me.

"One of my favorite books of all time is *Think and Grow Rich* by Napoleon Hill. When I first read that book, I was fascinated by the concept of unlimited possibilities, that everyone has a purpose, and how anything is possible in life. That completely inspired me.

"Today, my Personal and Spiritual Growth practices are at a whole different level than when I was in my early 20s but that's what makes it so exciting. It is a life long journey. There is always something new to learn and areas to expand."

~ Dave Lakhani ~
Author, Success Catalyst and Entrepreneur

"I was raised in a cult from age 6 until my late teens. I wasn't allowed to have any exposure to Personal Growth or any ideas that were outside of the group. The atmosphere was very controlling and domineering: There was corporal punishment for women who weren't subservient to their husbands, no education of women past the sixth or seventh grade, and no television or radio for anyone. The group wanted to cut off its members from anything outside of the group.

"I left the group in my late teens when I figured out what was going on. My search started with the study of persuasion: I wanted to understand how my mother was able to be a member of the cult and encourage her three sons to be part of the organization too. During my investigation, I discovered the Personal Growth industry.

"The first Personal Growth book that I read was Zig Ziglar's *See You at the Top*. It opened my eyes to developing new possibilities in my life. As a result, I became a tremendous fan of all kinds of Personal Growth work. I studied everything from Erhard Seminar Training (EST) when I was young to Neuro Linguistic Programming® (NLP®), of which I'm now a master practitioner.

"I have continued studying just about everyone who has come along in the industry. I've studied Anthony Robbins, T. Harv Eker, and other big names you've heard of for the purpose of finding answers to my questions about the nature of people and to expand options in my own life.

"Along the way, I became a teacher in the Personal Growth industry. I developed my own seminars around implementing critical thinking while being able to take action. I've found success as a trainer, while remaining a permanent student of Personal Growth."

Conclusion

These extraordinary, insightful, and compelling stories reflect the kinds of people you'll meet and experiences you'll have with Personal Growth.

Are you able to relate? It is clear that everyone has a unique journey. After reading these stories, I appreciate my life even more. In the past, I would think of my struggles as shortcomings and felt like a victim. Now I truly understand that everyone has their own journey and mine is perfect for me.

I feel blessed that Personal Growth is in my life—I don't know where I would be without it.

I encourage you to write down everything that was meaningful to you in this chapter. Make a commitment to yourself to integrate them into your life:

_____

_____

_____

_____

_____

_____

_____

_____

_____

_____

_____

_____

_____

3 What's Possible When More People Experience The Power Of Personal Growth?

> "If someone is going down the wrong road, he
> doesn't need motivation to speed him up. What
> he needs is education to turn him around."
> ~ Jim Rohn

> "Education is the most powerful weapon which
> you can use to change the world."
> ~ Nelson Mandela

Individuals and industry leaders alike seem to agree that the ripple effect of Personal Growth has a lifelong impact on society—some say it is small, while others say it is global. A society that understands the power of Personal Growth is closer than we think: In fact, it's already in the making.

Enjoy the following inspiring perspectives on what individuals and industry leaders see as possible when Personal Growth becomes a way of life: The realm of possibility and opportunities are now wide open.

~ Bud Harris ~

"People would smile more and thoughts would reflect what people wanted, rather than what they don't want. When you understand the Law of Attraction, you awaken to a world of new possibilities! When people exercise deliberate control over themselves, then life begins to be fun. When everybody in the world recognizes that nothing happens outside of their own creative control, the world will have an 'a-ha' moment."

~ Alexis Miller ~

"If more people had access to Personal Growth, there would be less crime, welfare, war, and chaos. In their place would be joy, happiness, and peace. Maybe people would even be able to take back some of the control from the government because people would feel more empowered in their own lives. Many would also be more willing to help others in need."

~ Fiona Johnson ~

"Can you imagine a place where smiles were the norm, the desire to pitch in was normal, and Personal Growth was a way of life? Can you imagine lives being lived where abundance and miracles were expected? Positive energy affects us; even when the sun doesn't shine, we do! The economy would be in a much healthier state if we didn't manifest all our bad habits."

~ Dave Ulloa ~

"Our world will become less medicated when people develop Personal Growth strategies, tools, and goals to overcome obstacles in life. In the future, I see people having more peaceful conversations that will lead to a more peaceful world. I see the growth in numbers of successful entrepreneurs breaking through limiting beliefs because Personal Growth has gone mainstream."

~ Edward Munoz ~

"We can have fewer divorces, more people out of jails, less crime, more kids graduating from high school and college, etc. With new leadership in place and citizens feeling empowered, I see the world improving with the help of Personal Growth. I call it 'The Tsunami Effect of Personal Growth.'"

~ Debbie Hoogestraat ~

"If Personal Growth became a way of life in society, the world would change for the better. We would think less about 'They have that, I want that, I can't have that, I am a victim.' Ungratefulness and envy create rifts and contribute to crime. Let's start by teaching others the truth: People have the power to change because they are the masters of their life and soul."

WHAT'S POSSIBLE WHEN MORE PEOPLE EXPERIENCE
THE POWER OF PERSONAL GROWTH?

63

~ Carolyn Ellis ~

"What I would love to see is more responsibility, integrity, and gratitude training in our education system: Character development as part of teacher training and in the classroom itself. Children learn concepts quickly. We need to teach them to address pressing environmental issues, like global warming, and encourage new political leadership to work collaboratively with other countries. Rather than stay stuck in adversarial mud-slinging, as Buckminster Fuller said over 60 years ago, we must move out of the 'independent/scarcity' mind-set into the 'interdependence/abundance' mind-set if we're to survive."

~ Daniel Durnam ~

"There is no question that we will soon experience a paradigm shift unlike anything seen before on this planet. Nothing will be impossible!"

~ Eric Turiansky ~

"If all my friends and family and the people I interact with on a daily basis were involved in Personal Growth, my world would be so different. We would speak the same language, understand each other better, and be more tolerant, knowing we enter into relationships with predefined expectations."

~ George Lodge ~

"If Personal Growth were a common practice in most people's lives, we would have less poverty, hunger, violence, war, crime, and hatred. Our society could be elevated to a much higher vibrational level—where people learned to be more accepting of themselves and others. We would all get along a lot better and be happier people."

~ Karen Walker ~

"People would be happier, be more successful, have more fulfilled lives, and encourage and support each other in a world where Personal Growth was a way of life. Competition, fear, and control would melt away worldwide."

~ *Julia Nelson* ~

"Personal Growth fosters relationships, which become more meaningful to us as they grow, flourish, and encompass the community."

~ *Paul Gruber* ~

"If Personal Growth became an integral part of our daily lives, in one year we would see fewer heart attacks and less obesity, poverty, hatred, and animosity. This is equivalent to a new world order over a short time."

~ *Monika Zands* ~

"If Personal Growth became a way of life it would expose truth and self-love, break down barriers between people, and teach us to revel in the beauty of our differences.

"Wouldn't it be great if we learned to work through differences and became empowered as a society? The industry gives a voice to our silence, allows space for our passion, and makes us feel safe about expressing our individuality. What's in store for the future? More faith, more love, more truth, and a life worth living."

~ *Lee Lam* ~

"In the future people will do jobs that suit them, rather than people doing jobs suited to their personal debts. We can create an amazing environment of positive energy, supporting each other and understanding differences between people. People will be happy with how they look or make changes for themselves and not because they feel they have to."

~ *Michael Abdalla* ~

"The world would be a much more fulfilling place with less fall-out from negative addictions if we could only achieve a better quality of life."

~ *Matthew Britt* ~

"Fear would fade in a world in which Personal Growth played a large role. People would gladly choose life over limitations."

WHAT'S POSSIBLE WHEN MORE PEOPLE EXPERIENCE
THE POWER OF PERSONAL GROWTH?

65

~ Venloe Scott ~

"The future with more Personal Growth will bring more love, acceptance and abundance."

~ Kathryn Arnold ~

"No doubt crime and war would be reduced, personal relationships and work relationships would flourish, divorce rates would lower, unemployment would decline; we'd have better communication in every area of our lives when Personal Growth becomes a way of life."

~ Lew Bronstein ~

"The awareness of Personal Growth has started to grow exponentially because people are beginning to realize that the status quo is unacceptable. I plan to touch as many lives as possible to facilitate growth. I know many people involved in the same endeavor to make Personal Growth a household word, which will expand and employ many people in the future.

"When Personal Growth has a place in society, crime will decrease and compassion will increase; the economy will thrive; stress and deprivation will lessen; and health will improve because of wellness and exercise programs and education. Pernicious stress will subside when people learn to understand themselves and each other, gaining control over their emotions, their lives, and their destinies. I see products increasing in quality and decreasing in price due to awareness, accompanied by pride in the workplace, and cooperation between management and workers. I foresee career changes as people go for what really matters. Many innovative businesses will result from their efforts. I see a possible increase in divorce for a short period followed by a drastic decrease in the divorce rate linked to people raising their standards and staying in relationships they want—not settling for lukewarm security.

"The future of Personal Growth is in creating accessible networks where people who desire the same lifestyle and hold similar beliefs can meet and share."

~ *Myndi Bogdanovich* ~

"If Personal Growth was commonly practiced, people would feel fulfilled in their daily lives. The benefits to society would be tremendous—people helping themselves, people helping others. This past Christmas, my husband and I were inspired by Oprah's Gift of Giving campaign, and instead of presents we gave each of our family members $50 in cash to give away to help make someone's holiday be a tiny bit easier. It wasn't life-changing, but the $900 we sent out into the world gave my family the opportunity to feel what it's like to impact someone's life in a positive way. We benefited greatly from the experience, and each of us had stories of our own to share about the experience."

~ *Kyle Brandt* ~

"When you know you've explored your own truth, you change. Anger and hostility would diminish in a society that embraced Personal Growth principles. I know that there are some in this world who will continue on their current path, but the majority of people would learn to live with respect and kindness because the reasons for their poor behavior would soon disappear."

~ *Mark Robinson* ~

"We could solve a lot of problems if people would look inside themselves and realize that growth is about us, not just me."

~ *Manny Goldman* ~
Author and Founder, PersonalGrowth.com

"Once people on a mass scale take responsibility for their lives and dedicate themselves to Personal Growth, I believe the global epidemic, which we've grown accustomed to accepting, such as global warming, homelessness, crime, poverty, obesity, and disease, will disappear.

One way to accelerate this is for those who currently know the power of Personal Growth to be willing to share it with their family, friends and colleagues.

"I see the future full of peace and happiness where people live the lives they only dreamed about. I see happiness, joy, and gratitude as the norm when Personal Growth becomes a widespread phenomenon – a way of life for everyone.

"It's now time to create the life we want, instead of reacting to the life we know that we don't want."

~ *Alison A. Armstrong* ~
CEO and co-founder of PAX Programs Incorporated

"When more people experience the power of Personal Growth, life will be stunning and the world a kinder and sweeter place.

"Personal Growth on a daily basis would be heaven on earth."

~ *David Riklan* ~
President and Founder of SelfGrowth.com

"People need to improve their relationships and how they interact with people. If you make a small positive change in your life and expand it to a global level you have the power to create a better world.

"Personal Growth on a daily basis means the better the world will be."

~ *Les Brown* ~
Author of the highly acclaimed and
successful book, *Live Your Dreams*

"As we move forward into the future and become more enlightened, there will be a shift in consciousness. We are going to realize that it is not about them or they anymore, it is about us and we. Only then will we have a much brighter world with less polarization and more innovation, more collaboration and cooperation within families, communities and governments on the local, national, and international levels.

"As we gain perspective, we realize that who I am is the same as who you are—and that makes us one. When we come to that realization, we will lock arms and turn to each other rather than turn on each other. We will become a blessing to the planet that I believe we are here to be."

~ Blair Singer ~
The Creator of SalesDogs®

"When Personal Growth becomes part of everybody's lives, there will be less whining, moaning, complaining, and finger-pointing.

"Schools of the future would teach children about communication, relationships, and how to manage all the little voices in their brains that may tell kids they're not good enough, how to deal with their emotions and how to deal with more complexity without the stress.

"Anybody who is ahead of the Personal Growth curve has an advantage when it comes to being a great employer, business owner, parent or investor. Personal Growth is the future—and we all know it.

"When *Time* magazine says that the Person of the Year for 2006 is 'You,' that tells you something. Personal Growth is already here.

"People are becoming more and more conscious about their personal evolution—this is the new wave. As complexity and choices increase most people realize that either you take ownership or become a victim. Personal Growth is a given."

~ Pat Finn ~
CEO, Rubicon Results Institute

"Look at everything that goes on in the world. Look at poverty and hunger. There are plenty of resources to feed everybody on the planet. Problems could be handled instantly, especially with a new paradigm on finances and money.

"When you take away the strife and stress, what's left is love. When you walk out of a Personal Growth event, you feel connected—you feel love. If the energy people put out were consistently positive, who knows what would be possible? It's certainly beyond my little brain to figure it out."

~ Clinton Swaine ~
Founder, Financial Frontier™

"The fastest way to create long-term success and peace on the planet is to have more and more people following a Personal Growth model.

"There would be more trainers, more books, and more exposure to Personal Growth for the average person.

"The future is truly exciting."

~ Jennifer S. Wilkov ~
Best-selling Author of *Dating Your Money*,
Publisher and Book Consultant

"When people wake up in the morning, they set the tone for their day.

"Personal Growth provides the opportunity for awareness for every single individual. The Golden Rule is: *Do unto others as you would have them do unto you.*

"As awareness for Personal Growth increases, society will continue to experience a rapid change. Over the next three years, the global community will progress on a deep level to influence, assist, and support the growth of individuals in many countries.

"We'll be able to turn to a complete stranger and say, 'How can I help you?' If someone at a restaurant drops a utensil on the floor, the person sitting next to him will say without thinking, 'Excuse me, may I pick that up for you?' That's a beautiful expression of what Personal Growth can cultivate in a person when the discipline becomes a way of life."

~ Spryte Loriano ~
Creator of livingDELICIOUS.com and
Founder of FEED333.com

"Personal Growth produces options. More people will grow to realize that they choose their life—all of it."

~ T. Harv Eker ~
Author of NY Times #1 Best-seller
Secrets of the Millionaire Mind™

"People are run by fear.

"If 1 billion or 5 billion people worked on themselves to alleviate their fears and anger, and they worked on developing love, oneness, unity, and unconditional acceptance, life as we know it would be transformed forever."

~ Cynthia Kersey ~
Author of *Unstoppable* and *Unstoppable Women*

"I absolutely believe that if we had a world of individuals who at a basic level possessed a consciousness that said, 'I'm truly responsible for my experience,' the world would start looking like a completely different place. That is the beginning of change and the foundation of my work."

~ Raymond Aaron ~
The Nation's Number #1 Success and Investment Coach

"Human energy and money could be put toward far more beautiful purposes that encourage compassion and help the lives of many people instead of focusing on unsolvable problems created to distract people from the truth."

~ Dave Lakhani ~
Author, Success Catalyst and Entrepreneur

"As a result of Personal Growth, intellectual capital will expand at an exponential rate. People will achieve what they want when they've clearly defined their missions and stay focused on them."

~ Larry Benet ~
The Connector

"If you see a homeless person on the street, instead of passing him by, you might ask that person what happened and what you could do to make a difference in his life. You would make a pretty powerful, profound statement in your life and impact on his life—and you'd be 'paying it forward.'"

~ W. Vito Montone ~
Co-Founder of BrandU®, Intention Products, and Prosperia

"Yes, there are side benefits to knowing oneself. As we work on ourselves, we can know one another better, and therefore achieve more. Then there will be a shift globally to what people would know as heaven on earth. This has begun."

~ Robert G. Allen ~
Best-selling Author of *Multiple Streams of Income*

"It would be a different world. People would get up in the morning feeling a lot more love, forgiveness, patience, and connection with a Higher Power. It would be a prosperous abundant world.

"Personal Growth is light. It takes time for some to see and feel it and it's delicious, magnificent, peaceful, and wonderful."

~ Lin Morel, MA, DSS ~
CEO, Beyond Words Group; Transformational
Women's Groups & Keynotes

"My sense is Personal Growth will grow exponentially. As a core group of individuals truly takes responsibility for themselves, they will become the new leaders. This group will be diversified by economic status, gender, race and culture—it is open to all.

"In the last 10 years, Personal Growth has gone from being the province of woo-woo hippies to everyday people who hire personal coaches, executive coaches, spiritual coaches, life coaches, and business coaches. You name it.

"There is a longing in people to connect to the answers to these questions: 'Why am I here? What am I to do to leave my mark on the world? Where am I going?' These are both Personal Growth and Spiritually based questions, and there is such an intertwining of the two. If people shy away from religion or spirituality, they'll embrace Personal Growth. To me, it's all the same thing: an unfolding of who we are and where we are going in this journey called life."

~ Jack Canfield ~
CEO, The Canfield Training Institute;
featured teacher in *The Secret*

"They say there's only one Earth. We won't get a second one. We can synergistically work together to create the greatest good for the greatest number of people.

"Everyone would be happier and healthier, and the economy would be much more robust. Everything would work better."

~ John Alexandrov ~
Author, Creator of The Money Chi Dotcom

"What will happen is more people are going to stand for something, instead of being against something. To me, that's a very important distinction upon which our future is dependent.

"Let's create a Personal Growth culture of ability, products, services, and technology so we can make significant changes in the world and encourage people to stand for something rather than be against everything."

Conclusion

Continue to explore what it would be like to live in a world of responsibility, accountability, education, communication, love, and peace where Personal Growth was a way of life for billions of people.

This paradigm shift is just the beginning of making authentic changes, a real difference, in our lives, in the lives of our loved ones, and in the global community.

I encourage you to write down everything that was meaningful to you in this chapter. Make a commitment to yourself to integrate them into your life:

_____

_____

_____

_____

_____

_____

_____

_____

_____

_____

_____

_____

_____

 Insights And Wisdom For Living

"Those people who develop the ability to continuously acquire new and better forms of knowledge that they can apply to their work and to their lives will be the movers and shakers in our society for the indefinite future."
~ Brian Tracy

"If you want to be successful, find someone who has achieved the results you want and copy what they do and you'll achieve the same results."
~ Anthony Robbins

There is a principle for success called *Modeling*, which is based on the idea that success leaves clues. In other words: Put yourself in a role model's shoes, adopt how he thinks, take action with what he does and how he does it, and you too will have a successful outcome.

I asked each person in the following chapter the principles they live by or teach that have made all the difference in their own and others' lives. It is truly amazing how affirmations, positive statements, and philosophies can motivate and inspire you to take action to produce concrete results in the real world.

If any of their concepts resonate with you, I invite you to consider applying what you have learned from them to your life. When you integrate their key insights and pearls of wisdom, you will see results.

~ Barbara Parker ~

"Emotion is created by motion: I can change my state of being through music and exercise. When I believe in myself, I make life happen—I attract what I want into my life. I have also learned that to fulfill myself, I need to be meeting my own needs for Personal Growth and contribution to the world."

~ David Sendroff ~

"There are a number of philosophies that I live by each and every day.

"My beliefs include: a Higher Power guides me; there is nothing more important than my health; I am either growing or dying; things are either adding value or taking it away; it's important to surround myself with the positive (thoughts, energy, people, music, movies, etc.) and move away from the negative; there is no such thing as failure—only feedback; I choose how I feel at any moment; I am at the cause of my life; and if I don't have something, it's because I don't really want it.

"Questions that I ask myself are: Is this healthy for my mind, body, and soul? How can I make this better? What can I learn from this?"

~ Lew Bronstein ~

"What's important in life: Creating a win-win for everyone; going to the finish line; having integrity; being positive and grateful; abstaining from negative/toxic thinking; minimizing my time with 'toxic' people; visualizations; and always finding creative ways to add value.

"You cannot fail unless you do not try; you have not failed if you learned something and apply it; and it is better to have loved and learned than to never have loved at all.

"Lastly, our children are the greatest gift from our creator and to the world: Love them, teach them, and make sure that they know you appreciate them!"

~ *Debbie Hoogestraat* ~

"The past does not equal the future. When I finally got this into my heart and soul, it freed me from excuses and criticism. Each moment is a choice and if I make a poor choice, I can make a new choice the next moment. I'm not tied to anything except my dreams."

~ *Tom Martin* ~

"Definition of personal responsibility: dropping any inclination to blame others (my parents, my employer, my spouse, or the government) for what's 'wrong' in my life. Ever since I stepped up to the plate for my own life, I've been happier, freer, and more successful than I ever imagined!"

~ *Matthew Britt* ~

"I care about trust, honesty, integrity, love, passion, friendship, honor, an open mind, and willingness to try new things. I always strive to do my best. I have learned that I cannot fail unless I quit and I know I will never fail because I won't quit!"

~ *Monika Zands* ~

"I live by open communication, honesty, and truth. I run my life with a high level of integrity: I do what I say I am going to do; I am who I say I am; and I can be relied on to act, create and discover. I believe that in order to love, I must love myself. The most successful principle I have followed is: Never go to bed without saying I love you. My husband and I have only been drawn closer in our marriage. We cherish our experience together and are clear about the commitment we have made."

~ *Karen Walker* ~

"Everyone is important and adds his own value in the world."

~ *Eric Turiansky* ~

"I know that nothing has any meaning beyond what I attach to it. Though this principle guides me in my life and shapes my life direction, I can honestly say that I have been guilty of falling out with my philosophies at times. Recognizing that it's OK is one of my greatest accomplishments."

~ George Lodge ~

"I live by the Law of Attraction, integrity, openness to possibility, and the Golden Rule: *'Do unto others as you would have them do unto you.'*"

~ Manny Goldman ~
Author and Founder, PersonalGrowth.com

"The core principles and philosophies I live by are very different from those I lived by prior to finding Personal Growth.

"Thanks to the awareness and knowledge I've experienced first-hand in Personal Growth, I have adopted new perspectives that have transformed my life for the better. I understand that I create my life through my thoughts, feelings, and actions. I also know that everything happens for a reason and those reasons serve to help me understand my life.

"I am extremely aware that both language and what I choose to focus on creates my reality. Who I spend my time with also shapes my destiny. There is an Anthony Robbins quote, which I think often about: *'The quality of your life is a direct reflection of the expectations of your peer group'.* Throughout my life I have seen the effects of that one!

"I always look to add value to people's lives. Who can I be, what can I do, and what can I say to help you? This one principle alone has contributed to the acceleration of my Personal Growth and business success. This is how I have built relationships with key industry leaders and individuals who have stepped up to support me. Always find creative ways to add value.

"I love the integrity in my life: whether it's being on time, doing what I say I would do, or keeping my word. Integrity brings me so much joy and attracts the most amazing people into my life.

"Another principle that guides my life is: Rather than the drive for money, I put my focus where my purpose is and this brings me great happiness. Congruent with my purpose, money becomes a by-product of my work—a result of the satisfaction I bring to others' lives. I believe that my financial net worth is a reflection of the positive contributions I am making in the world."

~ Les Brown ~
Author of the highly acclaimed and
successful book, *Live Your Dreams*

"In order to live a significant life and one you can be proud of, 'you must be willing to do the things today that others won't do in order to create and have tomorrow the things that others won't have.'"

~ Clinton Swaine ~
Founder, Financial Frontier™

"We're on the planet to learn about interaction and negotiation. Most people see the world in black and white—but it's a place of opportunity to share, communicate, express values, and negotiate.

"Every morning when I wake up, I look around and think: 'Wow, another great day to play on this incredible planet and create what I choose to create!' Taking ownership of what you create is powerful. With everything I do I ask: 'How can I impact the life of someone to make his life a little better?'

"Whether it's just smiling at someone at the airport, teaching my students about improving their lives, doing charity work, or teaching people health and nutrition through a network-marketing company—whatever I'm spending time on, I build positive relationships. The more I do this, the more I find my life getting better. The more I'm attracting everything that I want in my life, the more people I can impact."

~ Sarah Singer-Nourie ~
Founder, Singer Learning, Inc.

"Be. Do. Have. What do I want to HAVE out of this moment, day, year, experience, or program? What do I need to DO to make it happen?

"The most important question is: 'Who is it that I'm going to have to BE in order get where I want to go?'

"This means giving myself a lot of choices. For example, I could be a listener, a cheerleader, a model, or a partner."

~ *Alison A. Armstrong* ~
CEO and co-founder of PAX Programs Incorporated

"In business, we interact with our employees and bosses like they're misbehaving. We interact with our spouses and children like they're misbehaving.

"Mostly, when people are misbehaving we think that they're intentionally thwarting us, driving us crazy, and not giving us what we want. My philosophy is: what if no one was truly misbehaving?

"Adopting the point of view that 'no one is ever misbehaving' has given me the capacity to interact with people from a benevolent vantage point. I never blame.

"My philosophy makes me much more effective as an executive and as a teacher. By the way, I don't think my students or the leaders I'm training are misbehaving either. It certainly makes me a better mom and allows me to accept men, whom women generally regard as misbehaving most of the time.

"Some of my other philosophies are: Changing another person's life is a privilege. You never have the right to change a person's life without his permission. Everyone has unique gifts. Everyone has a place. If everyone had the freedom to pursue what he desired, it would all work out just fine.

"'People need to own their freedom to pursue their passions, interests, and loves.'"

~ *Jennifer S. Wilkov* ~
Best-selling Author of *Dating Your Money*,
Publisher and Book Consultant

"I live by the motto: 'Everyone wants to assist me with the life I want to live.'

"Whether a situation goes the way I expect or not, I am in a place where I acknowledge that everyone wants to assist me with the life I want to live.

"If I didn't get the deal, make the sale, or be given an incredible opportunity I think, 'Everyone wants to assist me with the life I want to live.'

"Another belief system I have consists of three words that occupy my waking moments and daily activities. They are:

"1. Prepare

"2. Prosper

"3. Protect

"When I do a beloved Shintaido martial arts workout, I prepare (warm up) and I prosper (incredible burn and air expansion in my lungs). I get an unbelievable feeling of being alive; I become invincible: a prosperity that is beyond words. Then, I protect (cool down) and give my body an opportunity to recover.

"This philosophy shows up in every area of my life: I use it in my work, relationships, and life.

"It is a simple philosophy, and I ask of others: How do they prepare? How do they prosper? How do they protect themselves and others impacted by their decisions and choices?

"Ralph Waldo Emerson's philosophy encourages me daily to continue my work and share my gifts with the world: *'Finish each day and be done with it. You have done what you could. Some blunders and absurdities have crept in. Forget them as soon as you can. Tomorrow is a new day. You will begin it serenely and with too high a spirit to be encumbered by your old nonsense.'*"

~ *Bob Burg* ~
Speaker and Author of *Endless Referrals*

"I don't believe in gossip, I believe in constant gratitude.

"Being gossip-free and living in extreme gratitude have made an absolutely, dramatically positive difference in my life."

~ Raymond Aaron ~
The Nation's Number #1 Success and Investment Coach

"I go to gratitude as often as I think of it, which is many times a day. When I'm in a relationship with a wonderful woman, I express my gratitude to her all the time. I'll call her during the day just to say I'm grateful. I sometimes start crying because I'm so grateful.

"When something 'bad' happens to me, I immediately go to gratitude to explore ways that what happened to me could be good, even if I don't believe it. I work at it until I get it."

~ Robert G. Allen ~
Best-selling Author of *Multiple Streams of Income*

"The first part of the day ought to be reserved for study and prayer.

"To audiences I ask, 'How many believe in a Higher Power?' Ninety-five percent of the people raise their hands.

"Most people say that a Spiritual practice is very important. If your Spiritual life is important, then prove it. Spend the first part of your day studying scriptures that are important to you. There are many great forms of scriptures from the Buddhist, Hindu, Muslim, and Christian perspectives. There is great wisdom in all of these books. If you study any of them, you will find great wisdom.

"Prepare your mind by reading for 20 or 30 minutes a day. Then do a soul-felt kneeling prayer. Clear your mind of all personal desires and problems and just say, 'Heavenly Father, help me make this a better day. What do you want me to do? How can I make this a better world?'

"For 55 years of my life, I didn't do that. In my 55th, year I learned to do it. I wish I had done that the previous 55 years. You will find possibilities opening up that seem miraculous.

"The second practice is to listen to your own true voice. Each of us has a true voice. Your mind processes information and creates solutions to problems. Your heart is a truth detector: It tells you whether what you're thinking is right or not. You feel whether things are right or not.

"Spiritual truth is a delicate process. If people had the courage to listen to their true voice, they would grow quickly. Most of the time, we make progress slowly because we spend time repairing the damage done by not following our intuition and true voice: We end up repairing the roads and paying off the debts because we haven't listened to our intuition.

"My intuition told me not to do a certain real estate project, and I just had to do it. I felt like I should, even though my intuition was very strong and said, 'Don't do this. It's not right now.' I went ahead and did it. It cost me 10 years of my life, $10 million, and a lot of lessons. It slowed me down dramatically. It forced me to build a very strong foundation. Now I make rapid progress with a stronger foundation.

"The third practice would be to discern between your critical voice and your true voice. There's a critical voice most of us have. When I interview my audiences I ask, 'How many of you have a critical voice?' Ninety-nine percent of the people raise their hands.

"What does your critical voice say to you? It says things like: 'You idiot, you're stupid. Who do you think you are?' Almost everyone's critical voice says this.

"You may have one foot on the gas, but your inner voice has its foot on the brakes. It doesn't want you to move forward. It beats you up for trying to make progress in your life. It talks you out of it, and then beats you up for not doing it. It's very insidious.

"The real question is: Who is that inner voice? Is that you? It's a very profound question. Next time you have a conversation with yourself, ask: 'Who is that voice? Is it mine? Why would I say those things to myself? Why would I try to damage myself in any way?'

"What is the voice? Is it you, your ego or whatever the psychologist wants to call it, or a Spiritual entity? I don't know, to tell you the truth. I have my hunches and hints, but I can tell you that inner critical voice is not your friend. The sooner you learn the inner critical voice is not your friend, the faster you can have Personal Growth.

"As soon as you learn that you have a deeper inner voice that is your friend, that does want you to win and grow, and when you learn to discern between those two voices and learn how to listen to one and manage the other, you have the basis for rapid Personal Growth in your life.

"If we learn to manage our critical and true voices, we will go wherever we choose."

~ Blair Singer ~
The Creator of SalesDogs®

"R. Buckminster Fuller was a great mentor for many people, including leaders like Mark Victor Hansen, Robert Kiyosaki, and myself...

"Fuller said that you may never know what your true purpose in life is, however, 'You can rest assured that you're fulfilling your purpose if you commit yourself to the highest advantage of others.'

"In other words, you may not know what your true purpose is, but as long as you commit to help people win, then you're probably doing what you're supposed to be doing.

"My guiding principle is, "How can I add the greatest value to the greatest number of people at the least cost and effort to them?" As a business philosophy, this forces you to grow big, be profitable, and continually add value to other people's lives.

"I was in the trucking business, the airfreight business, and the computer business. I'm now in the education and training business. My philosophy has always been the same for each business:

To create the greatest good for the greatest number of people with the least amount of effort and cost for them.

"Bucky Fuller talked about another principle: the concept of precession or ripple effect. In other words, when you drop a stone in water the ripples go out from the stone—the bigger the stone, the bigger the waves, the more stones, the more waves. In other words, everything you do has an affect on something else.

"He also talked about bumblebees' alighting on flowers in search of nectar for honey. What the bee actually does by getting pollen dust on its legs and moving from flower to flower is cross-pollinate the flora. The bees' purpose in nature is to cross-pollinate. If all the bees and insects disappeared, we'd have no plants!

"Bucky explains, 'Bees go out each day to make honey. We go out there to make money. They're honeybees and we're money bees. The difference between a bee and us is we've got a brain. The bee doesn't know that the ripple effect of their actions is cross-pollination. It just knows its own survival.' We have the choice to be conscious about our actions and the ripple effect of them.

"I take a look at how I can add more value, rather than just focusing on money. That is how we arrived at our mission statement, 'To improve the quality of life for everyone through transformation of the market place.' What is the ripple effect of those actions? If it adds more value it should bring in more money.

"The truth is that the bee ultimately figures out that the daisies over by the riverbank actually have a little bit more nectar in them than the roses over in the woods do. Bees start gravitating towards the daisies—then they find out that the taller daisies are a little bit better than the shorter daisies. By trial and error, a bee finds its niche. It becomes responsible for a certain type of honey as well as cross-pollinating a certain species of flower. It becomes very good at its job and fits in with the scheme of nature.

"I may never know what the perfect business is for me. But if you pay attention to the taps the Universe gives you on the shoulder and you add value to the lives of the greatest number of people at the least cost to them, you can rest assured that you're moving in the right direction. Money becomes a scorecard.

"If we weren't supposed to figure out how to work together, God, the Great Spirit, the Universe, whatever you want to call it, wouldn't have put six billion of us on one tiny little dirtball planet. I think that the purpose for all of us is to figure out how to make each other's lives better. We're supposed to continue to solve more and more problems together and raise the standard of living—happiness, health, and love for everybody.

"My principles have driven me for all these years and have provided me with incredible friends, relationships, and wealth."

~ Bill Bartmann ~
President, Bill Bartmann Enterprises

"Four words: 'Nothing bad ever happens.' This says to me that, yes, some calamitous things can happen, but not to worry.

"I've had many calamities and very significant tragedies. But in each and every instance, my wife, Kathy, and I have always been able to see some good in the bad. We don't always find it on day one or two—sometimes it takes a year or more before you look back and realize that you learned a good lesson. Bad experiences create great value, although at the time we're upset about them and it may be the saddest day of our whole life.

"Once you move away from trauma, you see and understand it more clearly. You can say: 'I did learn a lot. That taught me something. That helped me. I benefited. I got something out of that.'

"All of a sudden, the very thing that once upon a time was an extreme negative may in fact become a defining positive."

~ Larry Benet ~
The Connector

"I live by a couple of basic principles: When I meet someone, I get to know that person, figure out what is important to that person, see whether I can help the person or build a relationship to help him get whatever it is he wants. Either right on the spot or shortly thereafter, I assess what I can do to facilitate and help people.

"When I met Larry King, for example, I knew that the Larry King Cardiac Foundation was the most important experience to him. I presented some innovative fundraising ideas and introduced some wonderful people to the Larry King Organization—people who wanted to attend his annual gala event. It's about figuring out what's important to someone else, then helping him achieve desired results.

"Zig Ziglar says it best: *'If you help enough people get what they want, you'll obviously get what you want.'*

"Lastly, I try to share with people that it's not what you know, it's who you know. There is power in relationships."

~ Gary Ryan Blair ~
Best-selling Author and President of The Goals Guy

"My personal philosophy can be summarized into two words: Everything Counts!

"Everything Counts! offers a philosophy for running a great business and for enjoying a great quality of life. Its meaning is simple, yet powerful:

"Everything you say, every thought you entertain, and everything you do has a direction, which serves as an advance or a retreat in respect to your pursuit of excellence. Everything, regardless of size or intent has bottom-line consequences; therefore, everything counts—this is the golden rule of excellence.

"Everything Counts! is a call to greater personal awareness, accountability and self-discipline. It offers a fresh, honest perspective on living, an ongoing investigation of truth, and an investigation into how everything counts.

"A don't-sweat-the-small-stuff philosophy is flawed as it breeds poor customer service, under-performance, wasted opportunity, mistakes, inconsistencies, rework, and oversights.

"Ultimately the key to quality in life is doing little things correctly, all the time, every time, so that your every action produces a quality result. When each detail, no matter the size, is lovingly attended to, and each step in the process is given complete and careful attention, the end result will be inevitably of the highest quality.

"Self-examination grows into self-knowledge by paying attention to the words you use, reflecting on your thoughts, weighing your actions—this is part of the process you learn to master yourself. You shape yourself and develop your philosophies through observation and understanding of each moment. Selecting virtues over vices is crucial too."

~ Lin Morel, MA, DSS ~
CEO, Beyond Words Group;
Transformational Women's Groups & Keynotes

"I've looked at a lot of philosophies. I follow the philosophy of love because it transcends everything.

"Religions and philosophies boil down to a few things: One of these is that something greater than us exists. The paradox is that this greater something is also contained within us.

"Most of the religions and philosophies I've studied talk about love, being in the moment, and being responsible for your actions. Those are some of the philosophies that I follow. Every action has an opposite and equal reaction, which is a scientific principle. The Bible says, *'As you sow, you shall reap'*.

"The truth be told that if you can embrace life the way it is, you're in a whole lot better shape to deal with what exists in front of you. If life gives you grapes, for example, you don't wish you had lemons. You make grape juice.

"My philosophy is acceptance. It's gratitude for everything, no matter how challenging that is. I have an optimist's viewpoint.

When you lose something, a space is created that opens up for something new.

"We see things, but we don't really see things. If there are five people at the scene of an accident, you will hear five different stories on what happened. We must all learn to observe objectively. This is no easy task, as the very observation of something can change the outcome. Modern physics has already established this fact.

"What is constant in my life is my willingness to get up each time I fall and to know that there's a wonderful blue sky behind whatever clouds are there.

"Life is my journey: Whether it's uphill or downhill or I'm stuck in a dead end, it's still my journey. I'm always looking for the sunshine."

~ Sarano Kelly ~
Founder, The Game and Author,
The Game—Win Your Life in 90 Days

"The single biggest principle that I live by is the principle of oneness, which for me means being reflective.

"When I experience something that I don't understand, rather than my getting frustrated, angry, or question a particular incident or person, I question myself and ability to understand.

"I learned that principle early on as a child when my father, a minister, in church would say: *'Know the truth, and it will set you free'.*

"Of all the things worth striving for is understanding. In fact, I believe that we are entering an era of understanding, which has become possible because of all the misunderstanding in the world.

"When I see things in part, it forces me to consider: What would it look like if I had a much more holistic point of view?"

~ T. Harv Eker ~
Author of NY Times #1 Best-seller
Secrets of the Millionaire Mind™

"There are three keys I live by:

"1. Stay present. Be in the present: That's where real life is.

"2. Accept what is. Be able to accept what is and don't freak out because of imperfection.

"3. Make inner peace your priority. At some stage in life you want peace. If peace isn't a priority for you, you're going to find it very hard to be happy."

Conclusion

When you benefit fully from *The Power of Personal Growth*, you no longer have to spend the time and heartache figuring out life on your own. Who has the results you want? Study that individual closely, apply what you learn from him, and then get the outcome you have dreamed about.

I invite you to re-read this chapter several times and enjoy the process of integrating the key insights into your life. You will own the wisdom when you take action and live the knowledge.

I encourage you to write down everything that was meaningful to you in this chapter. Make a commitment to yourself to integrate them into your life:

_____

_____

_____

_____

_____

_____

_____

_____

_____

_____

_____

_____

_____

Epilogue

"Life is a succession of lessons which must be lived to be understood."
~Helen Keller

Thank you for reading this book.

I anticipate that you have gained valuable insights and wisdom and are now inspired to further continue your journey into Personal Growth. The bridge between the insights in this book and actually gaining the wisdom is to take action with what you learned. Please select a few key lessons to integrate immediately and watch your life soar.

It is my intention with this book to raise the global awareness of the power of Personal Growth for billions of people. As you make changes in your life, you will impact the lives of your loved ones and the world.

The popularity of the hit movie, *The Secret*, is a great example of how much the world is looking for change.

Some of the people we all look up to have stepped into the Personal Growth arena. Oprah Winfrey, one of the most influential women in America, launched a four-city tour in 2000 called *The Personal Growth Summit*. Her *O Magazine* is presented as "The woman's Personal Growth guide for the new century." Donald Trump, Richard Branson, Maya Angelou, Russell Simmons, and Michael Jordan, to name a few have written Personal Growth books and share their wisdom.

There are so many people teaching Personal Growth, addressing all areas of life. In 2008, we are launching our very special Virtual Courses. We will bring you the best trainers in every area of Personal Growth: health, relationships, finances, career, and more. Our courses are typically delivered via teleseminars, webinars and webcasts.

We will guide you through clarifying your mission and vision for your life and setting specific goals for the duration of the course. We custom build each course around the skills and knowledge you and the other students need to accomplish their outcomes.

Our exclusive VIP packages are available to help you maintain long-lasting results from your work during the classes. You will be provided with an accountability partner, mastermind groups, recordings of each session, access to an interactive online community, an in-person alumni live event and more.

With the purchase of this book, you have received a gift of two tickets to attend our life changing courses. Go to page 119 to learn more.

We owe it to the next generation to leave the planet in better shape than we inherited it. This mission starts with working on ourselves, which allows us to reach out and change lives. Everybody deserves to live in a world of love, joy, and abundance.

Join me in integrating Personal Growth into our daily lives. I encourage you to join our free online community at www.PersonalGrowth.com and interact with like-minded people dedicated to Personal Growth. I also welcome you to review the list of contributors in the book on pages 98 and 99 and explore what these amazing leaders have to offer.

In addition to the key insights and wisdom you have learned through **The *Power of Personal Growth***, I have compiled a list of 101 ways to experience Personal Growth – just for you. Follow the instructions on page 103 to creatively integrate Personal Growth into your life in so many ways. I'd love to hear which ones are most meaningful to you.

Share this book and its messages with family, friends, colleagues, and beyond…

Thank you.

with Love and Passion,

Manny Goldman
The Personal Growth Advocate™
Founder, PersonalGrowth.com
Author, *The Power of Personal Growth*

Contributors

Individuals...

Alexis Miller	Barbara Parker
Bud Harris	Carolyn Ellis
Daniel Durnam	Dave Razo
Dave Ulloa	David Sendroff
Debbie Hoogestraat	Edward Munoz
Eric Turiansky	Fiona Johnson
George Lodge	Judith Akins
Julia Nelson	Karen Walker
Kathryn Arnold	Korby Waters
Kyle Brandt	Lee Lam
Lew Bronstein	Mark Robinson
Matthew Britt	Michael Abdalla
Monika Zands	Myndi Bogdanovich
Nancy Brandt	Paul Gruber
Tom Martin	Venloe Scott

Industry Leaders...

For your convenience, please refer to
www.personalgrowth.com/resources to easily explore
the offerings from each of the industry leaders below.

Please note: Manny Goldman, Personal Growth Enterprises, Inc and our subsidiaries do not directly endorse the people and resources below.

Alison A. Armstrong
www.understandingmen.com
CEO and Co-founder of PAX
Programs Incorporated

Blair Singer
www.salesdogs.com
Creator of SalesDogs®

Clinton Swaine
www.financialfrontier.com
Founder, Financial Frontier™

Dave Lakhani
www.boldapproach.com
Author, Success Catalyst and
Entrepreneur

David "Avocado" Wolfe
www.davidwolfe.com
Author, Entrepreneur, and Raw
Food Expert

Jack Canfield
www.jackcanfield.com
CEO, The Canfield Training
Institute; featured teacher in *The
Secret*

Bill Bartmann
www.billbartmann.com
President, Bill Bartmann
Enterprises

Bob Burg
www.burg.com
Speaker, and Author of *Endless
Referrals*

Cynthia Kersey
www.unstoppable.net
Author of *Unstoppable* and
Unstoppable Women

David Riklan
www.selfgrowth.com
President and Founder of
SelfGrowth.com

Gary Ryan Blair
www.thegoalsguy.com
Best-selling Author and
President of The Goals Guy

Jennifer S. Wilkov
www.yourbookisyourhook.com
Best-selling Author of *Dating
Your Money*, Publisher and Book
Consultant

John Alexandrov
www.themoneychi.com
Author, Creator Of
The Money Chi Dotcom

Kim Castle
www.brandu.com
Brand Visioneer,
Co-creator BrandU®

Larry Benet
www.larrybenet.com
The Connector

Les Brown
ww.lesbrown.com
Author of the highly acclaimed
and successful book,
Live Your Dreams

Lin Morel, MA, DSS
www.linmorel.com
CEO, Beyond Words Group;
Transformational Women's
Groups & Keynotes

Pat Finn
www.rubiconresults.com
CEO, Rubicon Results Institute

Raymond Aaron
www.aaron.com
The Nation's Number #1 Success
and Investment Coach

Robert G. Allen
www.multiplestreamsofincome.com
Best-selling Author of
Multiple Streams of Income

Sarah Singer-Nourie
www.singerlearning.com
Founder, Singer Learning, Inc.

Sarano Kelley
www.saranokelley.com
Founder, The Game, and Author,
The Game - Win Your Life in 90 Days.

Spryte Loriano
www.livingdelicious.com
Creator of livingDELICIOUS.com
and Founder of FEED333.com

T. Harv Eker
www.peakpotentials.com
Author of NY Times #1 Best-seller
Secrets of the Millionaire Mind™

W. Vito Montone
www.wholewealth.com
Co-Founder of BrandU®, Intention
Products, and Prosperia

Vendors

Below you will find a majority of the vendors we used to complete the project.

Your Book is Your Hook
Jennifer S. Wilkov

Book consulting including our signature process for how to go From Thought to Sales in 90 Days™; Publishing; Guidance and stewardship to produce your book using ecologically sound resources; Business mentoring and Strategic Plans for Books

(718) 690-9669
www.yourbookisyourhook.com

The Admin Source, Inc.
Susie Ward

Print and digital book layout and design; transcription and editing

(301) 933-0616
www.theadminsource.com

Precision Mastery
Korby Waters

Coaching/Consulting (Professional and Business Excellence, Marketing, Direct Sales and Peak Performance)

(732) 762-2079
www.precisionmastery.com

Fulfillment Central
Brenda Zimbardi

Audio Services, Continuity Programs, Fulfillment and Distribution, Graphic Design, Internet Services, Marketing Materials Development, Duplication and Distribution, Variable Data Features for Personalization and Video Services

(678) 397-1302
www.fulfillmentcentral.com

Payson & Co., LLC
Payson F. Cooper

Custom Jewelry Design and Light Manufacturing

(212) 479-7942
www.paysonjewelry.com

Smart Office Solutions
Gregg Corella

Conference Calling, Web Conferencing, Replay Lines, Voice & Unified Messaging, Virtual PBX Phone Systems

(800) 891-8601 x112
www.smartofficesolutions.com

Intersect Inc.
Michael Heu

Graphic Design and Website
Design

(212) 260-1720
www.intersectnyc.com

Hartman Wildes
Angela Hartman

Public Relations and Event
Producer

(323) 650-9862

Success Media, LLC
Paul Hoffman

Empowering Music To Inspire...
Inspiring Words To Empower
"Live And Hear Life From A
Higher Vibration As YOU Create
Powerful Moments In Your Day"
Custom lyrics and complete songs
for authors, trainers and speakers.

(310)-568-3355
www.successsongs.com

90 Percent Attitude
Greg and Stephanie Mulac

Internet Marketing Consultants
providing Fast Track Mentoring
for Entrepreneurs and
Individuals seeking the Work at
Home Lifestyle.

stephaniemulac@gmail.com
www.elitecoachingclub.com

Cartoon Motivators
Richard Duszczak

Motivational Cartoons for purchase. We can create custom cartoons for your needs.

+44 (0)1246 209034
www.cartoonmotivators.com

Soto New Media Inc.
Mikaë Pilaprat

New Media and Design

(416) 849-1473

www.sotonewmedia.com

Carpe VM, LLC
Charles DeBenedittis

Video Advertising. (Marketing
consulting, project management,
storyboard design, videography,
editing, production of internet and
DVD media, distribution)

(212) 252-3326
www.carpevm.com

101 Ways to Experience Personal Growth

There are many forms of Personal Growth available to you at all times. Below is a list of 101 different ways that you can integrate it into your life right now. Whatever your experience is, there are several ways you can take your Personal Growth to the next level.

Everything you think, feel, say and do affects you, your loved ones and the global community. The world around you will automatically transform, as you continue to positively impact your life.

Enhance your Personal Growth today. Review this list and pick the top 3 choices to implement immediately. To see the results happen in your life, you must take action and now is the best time. Support others in your life by inspiring them to do the same.

Please refer to this list often. Continue integrating these into your life by finishing one and starting another.

1. Attend live events, seminars, workshops, retreats, and more

2. Listen to live and recorded teleseminars

3. Participate in live and recorded webinars

4. Listen to audio programs/books on CD, MP3, on the Web, etc.

5. Read books, special reports, newsletters, blogs, magazines, and more

6. Meditate

7. Exercise: gym, yoga, pilates, cardio, weight training, swimming, and more

8. Walk in nature or on the beach

9. Hire an expert as a coach (personal, business, physical trainer, and others)

10. Talk with a friend, loved one, colleague or a complete stranger

11. Journal

12. Visualize what you want

13. Create a vision board

14. Set and achieve goals

15. Take action on your goals and dreams

16. Be persistent in achieving your goals and dreams

17. Declare affirmations, make declarations and recite incantations

18. Set up a mastermind group(s)

19. Get an accountability partner(s)

20. Get a mentor

21. Become a mentor

22. Coach others

23. Teach others

24. Write a book, poem, music, etc.

25. Draw, paint, sculpt, sing, etc.

26. Have fun

27. Manage your time (schedule what's important to you first)

28. Learn from any situation in your life

29. Take 100% responsiblity for your actions and your life

30. Network

31. Spend time with empowering friends

32. Do what you love to do – work, recreation, hobbies, etc

33. Smile

34. Laugh often

35. Be optimistic

36. Go to the chiropractor before there is a problem

37. Relax on the beach

38. Travel

39. Speak with an elder

40. Spend time with babies and kids

41. Connect with God or your Higher Power

42. Spiritual and/or Religious rituals

43. Focus on your breath – deep diaphragm breaths

44. Apologize to someone

45. Forgive yourself and others

46. Face your fears and step out of your comfort zone

47. Educate yourself – find programs to develop skills and experience

48. Be happy

49. Focus on what you want

50. Connect and visit with loved ones

51. Discover and live from your purpose

52. Attitude of "Constant and Never Ending Improvement"

53. Model others - study people who have what you want

54. Be grateful for everything and everyone in your life

55. Write a list of everything you are grateful for

56. Watch inspirational movies, documentaries, and more

57. Surf the internet for valuable information

58. Go on a date

59. Schedule a date night with your significant companion

60. Study biographies of your role models

61. Say "I Love You" to someone

62. Have a heart to heart (deep and open) conversation with someone

63. Get a massage

64. Take a bath

65. Talk with a therapist or spiritual counselor

66. Garden

67. Call a friend or family member you haven't spoken to in some time

68. Create a life plan

69. Listen to music

70. Be spontaneous

71. Go to the spa

72. Feng Shui your home and office

73. Go dancing

74. Manage your finances

75. Be adventurous

76. Eat healthy

77. Buy organic food

78. Cook a meal

79. Do something that brings you joy

80. Play like you did as a child

81. Do outdoor activities – water sports, bike riding, and more

82. Ask someone for advice

83. Create a board of advisors for your life and/or business

84. Start a business – part time or full time

85. Pray

86. Relax

87. Spend an hr/day/week without distractions (cell phones, t.v., computers, etc.)

88. Just Be – be present to what is without having to do and say anything

89. Attend a networking event

90. Take a role model to lunch

91. Do something new you have never done before

92. Review circumstances from your past to discover what you've learned

93. Plan a romantic trip with your intimate partner

94. Take a drive in your car for pleasure

95. Set boundaries in your relationships and life

96. Tell others how you want to be treated

97. Identify your values and beliefs

98. Get clear on what's important to you and take a stand for it

99. Be in integrity and congruent with who you are

100. Invest in your future

101. Study history – the world and your family's

Please choose the top 3 forms of Personal Growth you will now integrate into your life:

Date: _____

_____   _____   _____

Quotes

Below is a list of most of the quotes mentioned throughout the book. I have consolidated them here for you to enjoy as much as I do.

"In times of change, learners inherit the earth; while the learned find themselves beautifully equipped to deal with a world that no longer exists."
~ Eric Hoffer

"The whole point of being alive is to evolve into the complete person you were intended to be."
~ Oprah Winfrey

"The only thing more expensive than education is ignorance."
~ Benjamin Franklin

"Every adversity, every failure, every heartache carries with it the seed of an equal or greater benefit."
~ Napoleon Hill

"The secret of life isn't what happens to you, but what you do with what happens to you."
~ Dr. Norman Vincent Peale

"If someone is going down the wrong road, he doesn't need motivation to speed him up. What he needs is education to turn him around."
~ Jim Rohn

"Education is the most powerful weapon which
you can use to change the world."
~ Nelson Mandela

"Those people who develop the ability to continuously acquire new and better forms of knowledge that they can
apply to their work and to their lives will be the movers
and shakers in our society for the indefinite future."
~ Brian Tracy

"If you want to be successful, find someone who
has achieved the results you want and copy what
they do and you'll achieve the same results."
~ Anthony Robbins

"Life is a succession of lessons which
must be lived to be understood."
~Helen Keller

"We are spiritual beings having a human experience."
~ Teilhard de Chardin

"When the student is ready, the master appears."
~ Buddhist Proverb

"The quality of your life is a direct reflection of
the expectations of your peer group."
~ Anthony Robbins

"If you help enough people get what they want,
you'll obviously get what you want."
~ Zig Ziglar

"Someone's opinion of you does not have to become your reality."

"Develop your communication skills, because once you open your mouth, you tell the world who you are."
~ Leroy Washington

"As you sow, you shall reap."

"Know the truth, and it will set you free."

"Faith comes by hearing and hearing and hearing."

"Do onto others as you would have them do unto you."

"Be ye not conformed to his world, but be ye transformed by the renewing of your mind."
~ The Bible

"Look at a man the way that he is, he only becomes worse. But look at a him as if he were what he could be and he becomes what he should be."
~ Johann Wolfgang von Goethe

"If I had eight hours to chop down a tree, I'd spend six hours sharpening my ax."
~ Abraham Lincoln

Resources

You can experience Personal Growth simply by walking in nature, meditating, exercising, setting goals, or finding lessons in life situations.

There are thousands of authors, speakers, and trainers who have mastered the key aspects of life. These amazing people show us how to have what we want in our lives. When you take the time to learn from others' mistakes and triumphs, you have a better chance at making good decisions for yourself and having a higher success rate.

There is a distinction between learning information and gaining the wisdom. The key is taking action: implementing the information into your life and accomplishing a result. Measure your outcomes and correct along the way. Be persistent and continue this process for as long as it takes to get the outcome you ultimately desire.

The Personal Growth industry is filled with extraordinary knowledge, which is shared in seminars, teleseminars, books, audiotapes, DVDs and more.

On the following pages are lists of the various people, resources and companies mentioned throughout this book. I have consolidated them here for your convenience and invite you to find out more about them.

Please note: Manny Goldman, Personal Growth Enterprises, Inc and our subsidiaries do not directly endorse the people and resources below.

People

Anthony Robbins

Bill Gates

Confucius

Denis Waitley

Dr. M. Emoto

Earl Nightingale

General Norman Schwarzkopf

Jim Rohn

Larry King

Maya Angelou

Napoleon Hill

Paul Hobby

Ralph Waldo Emerson

Robert Kiyosaki

Russell Simmons

Zig Ziglar

Barbara Walters

Bobbi DePorter

David Schwartz

Donald Trump

Dr. Martin Luther King Jr.

Eric Jensen

Henry Ford

Joseph McClendon III

Mark Victor Hansen

Michael Jordan

Norman Vincent Peale

R. Buckminster Fuller

Richard Branson

Robert Schuller

Sensei, H. F. Ito

Books

Awaken the Giant Within by Anthony Robbins
Psycho-Cybernetics by Maxwell Maltz
See You at the Top by Zig Ziglar's
The Laws of Success by Napoleon Hill
The Magic of Thinking Big by David Schwartz
The Monk Who Sold His Ferrari by Robin Sharma
Think and Grow Rich by Napoleon Hill

Audio

Get the Edge® by Anthony Robbins
Lead the Field by Earl Nightingale
Little Voice Management System™ by Blair Singer
Personal Power® II by Anthony Robbins
The Power of Positive Thinking by Dr. Norman Vincent Peale
The Strangest Secret in the World by Earl Nightingale

Films
The Secret
What the Bleep do We Know?!™

Programs

Anthony Robbin's
-Mastery University®
-Leadership Academy®
-Unleash the Power Within
-Date with Destiny®

EST (Ernard Seminar Training) – Currently Landmark
Education
- Landmark Forum

Jennifer Wilkov's *Your Book Is Your Hook™* workshop

Marshall Thurber's *Money & You*

Mind Power by John Kehoe

SuperCamp® by Quantum Learning Network™

T. Harv Eker / Peak Potentials Training
-Millionaire Mind Intensive
-Quantum Leap

Companies / Not for Profits

American School for Japanese Arts

Landmark Education

Larry King Cardiac Foundation™

National Speakers Association®

Oral Roberts University

Peak Potentials Training

Toastmasters International

Other

Hypnosis® and Time Line Therapy®

Law of Attraction

Neuron-Linguistic Programming (NLP)®

O Magazine

Shintaido (type of martial arts)

Time Magazine

Toastmasters International

Verbal Judo

Speakers Hall of Fame

Scriptures
 -Buddhist
 -Hindu
 -Muslim
 -Christian

About the Author

An entrepreneur, visionary and advocate for Personal Growth, Manny Goldman has been transitioning and transforming his life since he was 12 years old. His passion for Personal Growth is fueled by the amazing results he experienced in his own life and in the ripple effect on the lives of his loved ones.

Manny has seen the highs and lows of entrepreneurship and life in general. At age 19, he took over his family's business when his father was unable to work. Then he started a series of companies over the next 3-1/2 years. Eventually, he lost everything when the primary company was subsequently shut down by the New York Attorney General. His company was down for the count, and so was Manny. He was 50 pounds overweight, clinically depressed, in debt for more than $100,000, and lost with what to do with his life.

Following his first exposure to Personal Growth, Manny released the weight and the depression and became passionate about life. Over 3 years, he has become an avid student of Personal Growth, attended and volunteered at more than 50 seminars, read dozens of books, and listened to countless audio programs.

Today, Manny is married to his soul mate, lives in paradise (Santa Monica, CA) and is living his purpose. He gathered his wisdom for living through integrating the insights he learned throughout his experiences. Every day, he meditates, writes in his journal and walks in nature to further integrate his Personal Growth.

He believes that Personal Growth can transform the world one person at a time. His mission is to raise the global awareness of the power of Personal Growth for billions of people.

To order additional copies of
The Power of Personal Growth, please go to:
www.PersonalGrowth.com

To book Manny for a speaking engagement, please call (310) 230-5185 and email speaking@PersonalGrowth.com.

Special Bonus Offer

With the purchase of this book you have received a special gift of two tickets to attend our life-changing Virtual Courses. Our courses will be delivered via teleseminars, webinars and webcasts.

We will bring you the best trainers in every area of Personal Growth: health, relationships, finances, career, and more. We will guide you through clarifying your mission and vision for your life and setting specific goals for the duration of the course. We custom build each course around the skills and knowledge you and the other students need to accomplish their outcomes.

Our exclusive VIP packages are available to help you maintain long-lasting results from your work during the classes. You will be provided with an accountability partner, mastermind groups, recordings of each session, access to an interactive online community, an alumni in person live event and more.

Our programs will begin in 2008. For more information and to register, go to www.PersonalGrowth.com and click on the "Courses" link.

If you have no access to a computer, call toll free 1(866)694-GROW (4769)

---

* The offer is open to all purchasers of **The Power of Personal Growth** by Manny Goldman. Original proof of purchase is required. The offer is valid for our Virtual Courses only. The value of this gift for you and a companion is $2,390, as of November, 2007. There is an additional fee for our VIP packages. Corporate or organizational purchasers may not use one book to invite more than two people. While admission to the program is complimentary, participants will be responsible for their telephone and internet costs. Participants in the courses are under no additional financial obligation whatsoever to Personal Growth Enterprises, Inc., Manny Goldman or any of our subsidiaries. We reserve the right to deny entry and ban anyone we believe may disrupt the course in any way.

Submit Your Story

Do you want to be included in the next edition of *The Power of Personal Growth*?

By submitting your story and contributions to us, you will impact other people's lives who read it for centuries to come. We are particularly seeking stories about people who have grown beyond extreme circumstances and challenges, thanks to Personal Growth.

Please answer these following questions:

1. What is your definition of Personal Growth?

2. Please share a compelling story about your life before you found Personal Growth, how you found it and your life now as a student.

3. How do you envision our world as more people experience the power of Personal Growth?

4. What philosophies, insights and wisdom can you share which have made all the difference for you in your life?

5. What are the top 3 Personal Growth resources that have made the most difference for you? (i.e. specific books, seminars, audio programs, etc.)

6. What are your top 3 favorite ways to experience Personal Growth? (i.e. seminars, meditation, reading, walking in nature, and more.)

Send the answers to these questions along with your name and contact information to stories@PersonalGrowth.com.

Please direct all questions and concerns to support@PersonalGrowth.com

If you are a Personal Growth industry leader, we would prefer to do an interview with you. Please email us your website address and contact information to stories@PersonalGrowth.com.

Thank you.

Index

Charity

Personal Growth Press, Inc. is proud to donate 10% of the proceeds of *The Power of Personal Growth* to charity. We support the people who typically aren't aware of Personal Growth and may not know how to access it including children, the homeless, prison inmates, single parents, start up entrepreneurs and more.

For Personal Growth to truly be a way of life for billions of people, it is important for everyone to have the ability to benefit from it too.

If you are passionate about a particular charity that is aligned with our mission of making Personal Growth a way of life for billions of people, we welcome you to provide us with the following information:

- Name of the charity

- Brief description of their cause

- Why you feel it is aligned with our mission

Please send your email to charity@personalgrowth.com.

Thank you.

PersonalGrowth.com

Join me in integrating Personal
Growth into our daily lives.

I encourage you to join our *free* online community at:

www.PersonalGrowth.com

Interact with like-minded people dedicated to
Personal Growth.

When you join now, you will have access to member
profiles, forums, groups, messaging, and much more…